Carlo Gébler was born in Dublin in 1954. He is a graduate of the University of York, where he studied English Literature, and of the National Film and Television School. His recent work includes *The Cure* (1994) and *How to Murder a Man* (1998) as well as the short story collection *W.9 & Other Lives* (1996). His version of Strindberg's play cycle, *Dance of Death*, was published by Lagan Press in 1999. His most recent publication is a memoir of his father, *Father & I* (2000). Currently writer-in-residence, H.M.P. Maghaberry, Co. Antrim, he is married with five children and lives outside Enniskillen in Co. Fermanagh.

By the same author

Fiction
The Eleventh Summer
August in July
Work & Play
Malachy and His Family
Life of a Drum
The Cure
W.9 & Other Lives
How to Murder a Man

Non-Fiction
Driving Through Cuba: An East-West Journey
The Glass Curtain: Inside an Ulster Community
Father & I

Children's Fiction
The TV Genie
The Witch That Wasn't
The Base

Young Adult Fiction
Frozen Out
Caught on a Train

Drama
Dance of Death

10 ROUNDS

10 ROUNDS

an adaptation of Arthur Schnitzler's La Ronde

CARLO GÉBLER

LAGAN PRESS
BELFAST
2002

The author gratefully acknowledges the financial support of the *Arts Council/An Chomhairle Ealaíon.*

For performance permission inquiries, please contact Antony Harwood, Office 109, Riverbank House, Putney Bridge Approach, London SW6 3JD, England.

Published by
Lagan Press
138 University Avenue
Belfast BT7 1GZ

Arts Council logo

ISBN: 1 873687 44 3
Author: Gébler, Carlo
Title: 10 Rounds
2002

Set in New Baskerville
Printed by Noel Murphy Printing, Belfast

To the cast and all at the Tricycle Theatre

10 ROUNDS

10 Rounds was first performed at the Tricycle Theatre, London on 23rd September 2002. The play was directed by Nicolas Kent. The cast was as follows:

Prostitute	Mairead McKinley
Volunteer	Des McAleer
Au Pair	Victoria Smurfit
Student	Michael Colgan
Wife	Clare Holman
Husband	Tim Woodward
PR Girl	Victoria Smurfit
Academic	Des McAleer
Spokeswoman	Brid Brennan
Official	Stephen Boxer
Designer	Poppy Mitchell
Lighting	Matthew Eagland
Sound	John Leonard
Production	Shaz McGee

10 Rounds was commissioned by the Tricycle Theatre, London, with the help of a grant from Bloomberg LP.

THE TIME: A scorching summer at the end of the twentieth century.
THE PLACE: Northern Ireland.

1 THE PROSTITUTE AND THE VOLUNTEER
Late in the evening. Red light district, Belfast.

PROSTITUTE: Oi!

VOLUNTEER: What?

PROSTITUTE: Where are you going?

[*He turns and smiles.*]

VOLUNTEER: That's none of your fucking business.

PROSTITUTE: Oh, we've got a way with words, I see.

VOLUNTEER [*lightly*]: I'm in a rush. I've things to do.

PROSTITUTE: It won't take long. I'll rephrase that. Stay and enjoy me.

VOLUNTEER [*suddenly interested*]: What are we talking?

[*She holds her fingers up.*]

PROSTITUTE: That's a very good price.

VOLUNTEER: All right.

[*He pays.* PROSTITUTE *stows his money in purse that hangs on a string arranged crosswise across her chest.*]

PROSTITUTE: Plus the cost of the hotel.

VOLUNTEER: That isn't part of the deal.

PROSTITUTE: Yes, it is.

VOLUNTEER: No, it isn't.

PROSTITUTE: It is. Where do you think I do it?

VOLUNTEER: Round there, behind the wall.

PROSTITUTE: It smells of piss.

VOLUNTEER: Round there, against the wall, or nothing. I haven't time.

PROSTITUTE: No.

VOLUNTEER [*grabs purse*]: I'll have my money back.

PROSTITUTE: All right. Another note. And a drink.

VOLUNTEER [*slaps her palm*]: Done. Right, let's go. I haven't got all night.

PROSTITUTE: Where's the rest of the money?

[*He steers her towards the wall.*]

VOLUNTEER: Don't be stupid. You think I'd cheat you of a few paltry quid. Jesus, woman, I'd sooner sell my granny.

[*They disappear behind the wall. We can only hear them now.*]

PROSTITUTE: Watch it, we've got to be careful. One slip behind here and we're in the Lagan.

VOLUNTEER: That would be interesting.

PROSTITUTE: Don't be a twat. This skirt's worth a night's work and I can't swim.

VOLUNTEER: I can. I could save you. I could give you mouth to mouth. I done First Aid you know.

PROSTITUTE: Oh yeah.

VOLUNTEER: Right, get yer kacks off.

PROSTITUTE: Hang on, will you. We're not catching a plane here.

VOLUNTEER: I really haven't all night.

PROSTITUTE: I haven't either. No, hold these. Right, ready. Come on, boy.

VOLUNTEER: Oh God. Oh Jesus. Oh yes.

* * *

VOLUNTEER *and* PROSTITUTE *come out from behind the wall.*

PROSTITUTE: It'd have been a lot better in a hotel. It's minging behind there.

VOLUNTEER: Short and sweet, that does me, thank you very much.

[*She steps into her knickers. He lifts her skirt and looks at her bottom.*]

PROSTITUTE: Do you mind!

VOLUNTEER: 'Made in Ulster'. Nice tat.

[*She pulls her knickers up.*]

PROSTITUTE: It was Portrush. I was fourteen, pissed. I didn't know better.

VOLUNTEER: What is it with your lot and tats? I've never understood.

[*She straightens her clothes and steps up to him.*]

PROSTITUTE: I've had plenty of youse with 'Made in Ireland' so don't start.

VOLUNTEER: Fair enough.

PROSTITUTE: My name's Leonie-Anne. I think you should tell me yours.

[*He chuckles.*]

VOLUNTEER: I'll be seeing you.

PROSTITUTE: Hang on. You owe me. I want another note.

VOLUNTEER: Oh aye. Course I do. I wouldn't want you to think I'm one of those.

PROSTITUTE: One of what?

VOLUNTEER [*hands note over*]: Those men who have it and then don't pay.

PROSTITUTE: Oh aye, those. Well, I didn't have you down as one of them.

VOLUNTEER: Am I to take that as a compliment?

PROSTITUTE [*stows money in purse*]: Aye, you do that.

VOLUNTEER: Isn't that risky, a purse on a string? Someone could cut it off.

PROSTITUTE [*pulling cord so purse disappears behind*]: I go like that, purse goes behind. Outside, like now, back to the wall, no one could get it.

VOLUNTEER: What about in a hotel? Don't you strip off?

PROSTITUTE: That's different. There I give it to the doorman to hold. I know most of them in the city centre. Or another girl. There's always someone I know in the foyer. You wouldn't want to take your money into a room with a strange man.

VOLUNTEER: What do you think about?

PROSTITUTE: When?

VOLUNTEER: You wouldn't get any pleasure from this, would you?

PROSTITUTE: Oh no. You think about other things.

VOLUNTEER: Oh great.

PROSTITUTE: It's after I look forward to.

VOLUNTEER: The relief is it?

PROSTITUTE: Some of them, they talk. You hear some quite interesting stories. I listen. I like to talk as well. Those are what I do better than anything, listening and talking. Should have been a social worker, shouldn't I? [*She laughs.*]

VOLUNTEER: What about just now? What were you thinking then?

PROSTITUTE: Actually, I was thinking about my father. He'd play this game. He'd clench his fist and fifty pence'd be in it. If I could open his fingers I could have it. I never did manage. He was a farmer. He had very strong hands. He came into my mind because he had this sharp chemical smell. Fertiliser. You have it too.

VOLUNTEER: I'm away here.

PROSTITUTE: What about that drink?

VOLUNTEER: Do you like your nose?

PROSTITUTE: I do, yeah.

VOLUNTEER: Any more fertiliser cracks, I'll take a Stanley to it.

[*He starts to walk away.*]

PROSTITUTE: Don't be angry, mister. I'm just trying to be friendly. All I want is regulars. You and me, same place, same time …

VOLUNTEER: See that. That's the thumb I use with my Stanley. Now wise up, girl.

[*He leaves.*]

PROSTITUTE: I only asked a bit of attention. But could you give it? You're all the same you ones, so you are. You all talk big about the people but when the chips are down, you're crap. [*He returns holding up his thumb.*] The beast in the field has more feelings than you.

[PROSTITUTE *runs off.* VOLUNTEER *goes the other way.*]

2 THE VOLUNTEER AND THE AU PAIR

Storeroom of the Ernie O'Malley Republican Club. Kegs and crates everywhere. A baseball bat and tools in the corner. A door opens. Sounds of revelry and music from the club beyond. AU PAIR *comes in. She wears a Palestinian scarf and expensive glasses.* VOLUNTEER *follows. He closes the door behind him, then deftly wedges baseball bat under handle. He's done this before.*

AU PAIR: What's this?

VOLUNTEER: It's the Stew Room.

AU PAIR: Did you say screw?

VOLUNTEER: There's another reason to hate the fucking Brits, the bloody language, so many words sound the same. No, darling, I didn't say screw. I said stew. Stew—say stew.

AU PAIR: Stew.

VOLUNTEER: Stew. Enjoy it. Roll it round your mouth. Stew.

AU PAIR: I don't know this word.

VOLUNTEER: When you stand tea in a pot on the stove it stews.

AU PAIR: This is for tea making and drinking?

VOLUNTEER: No, nothing to do with tea. Forget I ever mentioned tea.

AU PAIR: Okay, tea gone. Anyhow, I don't know tea. I am drinking coffee.

VOLUNTEER: Can't abide the stuff myself, makes me sick as a dog.

AU PAIR: Oh, so sad, it is lovely drink.

VOLUNTEER: So I've been told.

AU PAIR: So why stew room? You mean store maybe? This is beer store?

VOLUNTEER: Let me explain. When we have a young man in the area who isn't behaving properly, we bring him here. We sit him down. We have a nice long chat. We put him right. We tell him breaking into this wee woman's house, or driving off with that wee man's car, the community doesn't like it. Then we turn off the light and close the door and leave him in here to think about it. After a couple of hours stewing he usually sees things our way.

AU PAIR: You do that yourself?

VOLUNTEER: Aye, I'm a guardian. Where do you come from?

AU PAIR: I told you, Nürnberg.

VOLUNTEER: So you did.

AU PAIR: I suppose you've forgotten my name as well?

VOLUNTEER: Heidi. How could I forget that?

AU PAIR: Oh, very good! I am impressed. You Irish man are not like man in Germany.

VOLUNTEER: Pigs, are they?

AU PAIR: They just want, you know, to have their way. No talking, no …

VOLUNTEER: Seduction?

AU PAIR: Exactly. They just …

VOLUNTEER: Ride roughshod?

AU PAIR: We don't want wallflower men, always asking, shall I do this, shall I do that? A man has to be a man. This I understand. But he has to be polite. He has to be charming. He has to be ...

VOLUNTEER: A bit like myself, you mean.

AU PAIR: Like yourself; yes, I would say so. Talk to me, dance with me, drinks with me ...

VOLUNTEER: Where are you living?

AU PAIR: South Belfast.

VOLUNTEER: And what are you doing, here?

AU PAIR: Little boy, three years old. I look after.

VOLUNTEER: Rich are they, your family? Must be where they live.

AU PAIR: No, middle class, nothing special, second marriage for husband, son from first marriage living at home also, though he seems to have room near university, two cars, money yes, but nothing exceptional.

VOLUNTEER: Snobby people are they?

AU PAIR: Snobby?

VOLUNTEER: Stuck up, distant?

AU PAIR: He's a bit cold. He's a judge. I suppose sitting in court all day you'd have to be. But he's nice really. I like him.

VOLUNTEER: Cigarette? [*He proffers a box.*]

AU PAIR: Yes.

[*They sit on crates and light up.*]

VOLUNTEER: What brought you up here then? Fancied a bit of rough like me, did you?

AU PAIR: I read, you know, before I come to Northern Ireland. I'm learning this side of the city is so important. So, free night, I come over, meet Sharon and Kelly and Debbie in pub and they bring me here, and I meet you. Very nice, very friendly people here in west but also it's centre of the struggle and I like to see for myself. I like to meet people who are part of struggle.

VOLUNTEER: You're a Troubles tourist?

AU PAIR: A tourist? No, I'm not a tourist. I'm not someone who comes, looks, goes. If I was that person, I wouldn't be here, I'd be on a beach.

VOLUNTEER: Of course, you want to know about things. Go into them. In depth.

AU PAIR: Yes.

VOLUNTEER: Well, now's your chance. I'm your man. Ask away.

AU PAIR: You're not a stranger to the struggle, I think.

VOLUNTEER: Everybody on that dance floor would know somebody shot or somebody injured or somebody lifted. You can't live here and not be touched. It would be impossible.

AU PAIR: And it is true what girls are saying? The British soldiers shoot you ten times?

VOLUNTEER: Oh aye.

AU PAIR: So this is why they're calling you ... ?

VOLUNTEER: Aye, Ten ... Ten Rounds Milligan, that's me.

AU PAIR: Light me please I'm out. [*He relights her cigarette.*] You are involved? You are volunteer?

VOLUNTEER: That would be saying.

AU PAIR: I think you are.

VOLUNTEER: Well, if that makes you happy—yes, I am.

AU PAIR: So why? Revenge for shooting you?

[*He laughs.*]

VOLUNTEER: No. A better world.

AU PAIR: And this you can do even with violence?

[*He laughs.*]

VOLUNTEER: 'You can't make an omelette without breaking eggs.' The man this club's named after said that.

AU PAIR: Eggs?

VOLUNTEER: Before making comes breaking.

AU PAIR: Ah.

VOLUNTEER: And you know what the tragedy is? There's a lot more fucking eggs to break yet.

AU PAIR: But there is ceasefire, I thought.

VOLUNTEER: Yeah, and there's the Agreement, but they're both cons ... [*He throws his cigarette aside.*] Speaking of breakage, give me your glasses. [*She hands her glasses to him.*] They look like they cost a few pounds. We wouldn't want to snap these would we? [*He puts her glasses carefully to one side.*]

AU PAIR: But now I can't see and I liked looking.

VOLUNTEER: It's not seeing me you should be thinking about.

[*He takes her cigarette, throws it aside and kisses her.*]

AU PAIR: What's that smell?

VOLUNTEER: What smell?

AU PAIR: Are you a farmer? That's a farm smell, isn't it?

[*His hands start to wander.*]

VOLUNTEER: I'm a city boy, darling. I hate the country. Nothing but field after fucking field. Give me tarmac any day, the more the merrier.

AU PAIR: Perhaps somebody comes in and sees us?

VOLUNTEER: You needn't fret, darling, no one'll come in.

AU PAIR: How do you know?

VOLUNTEER: I'm the main man here. This is where I do my thing. I'm the master of the Stew room.

***

AU PAIR: I can't see.

[*He hands her glasses to her.*]

VOLUNTEER: Did the earth move? It did for me all right. [*She does not move.*] You can't lie there all night.

AU PAIR: You like me do you?

VOLUNTEER: Oh aye.

AU PAIR: And you will bring me home?

VOLUNTEER: Not straight off, like. There's a lock of drinks with my name at the bar. I want to get them down my neck first. But of course I will later. I'll personally put you in the back of a cab and what's more I'll sit in beside you. We'll go all the way across town to your judge's house and I'll personally see you through the gate, along the path, right up to the front door. And I'll personally kiss you goodnight.

AU PAIR: Promise?

VOLUNTEER: Aye, you can trust your mate, Ten.

[*He holds out his hand. She takes it. He lifts her to her feet.*]

AU PAIR: Can I see you again?

VOLUNTEER: For sure.

AU PAIR: Tomorrow?

VOLUNTEER: I haven't got my diary. I'm a busy man.

AU PAIR: Next weekend?

VOLUNTEER: That might be hard. I may have to go up the country.

AU PAIR: But you hate the country.

VOLUNTEER: Tell me about it.

AU PAIR: So, when do we meet? There's so much I want to speak of.

VOLUNTEER: Don't worry. We'll work something out. [*He removes the keg and bat and opens the door wide. Laughter and amplified*

music is heard.] Come on, life's too short to mope. Put your
bright face on, girl, and dance.
[*He takes her by the waist and spins with her out into the club.*]

3 THE AU PAIR AND THE STUDENT

South Belfast. A well-appointed kitchen. Sun streams in. AU PAIR *sits at
the table reading out the letter she's been writing.*

AU PAIR: Last night I felt a very special feeling between us, a very
    unique … connection …
    [STUDENT *has crept in through the door without her realising.*]
STUDENT: Gotcha!
    [*He squeezes* AU PAIR *round the waist.*]
AU PAIR: Mensch, was machst du da?
STUDENT: It's only me.
AU PAIR: Don't do that. You gave me terrible fright.
STUDENT: Sorry, I was only messing.
AU PAIR: My heart, think what you've just done to it.
STUDENT: What you've done to mine is a lot worse, I can tell you.
    What's happening? What are you doing?
AU PAIR: Writing.
STUDENT: What? A list?
AU PAIR: No, a letter.
STUDENT: Is it for me?
AU PAIR: No.
STUDENT: You're writing home?
AU PAIR: No. With mother I always phone.
STUDENT: In which case it must be a man—so who is he?
    [*He cranes over table to read the letter.* AU PAIR *turns it over to stop him.*]
AU PAIR: How are you here?
STUDENT: Sorry, that sentence isn't quite up to scratch.
    [*He mouths, 'Why are you here?'*]
AU PAIR: Why are you here?
STUDENT: Good, keep talking.
AU PAIR: I thought you were at college today. That's what your
    father said.
STUDENT: He's right, I am, or I was. But that was then and this is

now. School's out for summer ... and I'm ready to rock and roll. [*He grabs* AU PAIR'S *arms and pulls.*] Come on. Let's dance. [AU PAIR *lets him pull her to her feet. They dance a couple of steps.*]

AU PAIR: No, stop. I can't. My head hurts. I'm having hangover.

STUDENT: Heidi, I'm sorry, you're here to learn English. I can't allow that. I am hungover. [*He looks into her eyes.*] I am hungover. Go on, say it.

AU PAIR: I am hungover.

STUDENT: Or, I have a hangover.

AU PAIR: I have a hangover.

STUDENT: Hangover.

AU PAIR: Hangover.

STUDENT: Hangover.

AU PAIR: Hangover.

STUDENT: I love you.

AU PAIR: I love ...

STUDENT: Alternatively, if you don't like 'hangover', try 'arseholed'.

AU PAIR: Arseholed?

STUDENT: Arseholed, as in I am completely.

AU PAIR: I am not arsehole.

STUDENT: Of course you aren't. You're absolutely wonderful. Your skin is clear. Your eyes are bright. Your ankles are perfect.

AU PAIR: Not a bit, how do you say?

STUDENT: Heavy?

AU PAIR: Yes, my mother used to say they were heavy but then my ...

STUDENT: Mother was a bourgeois fascist who resented that your father loved you more than her. [AU PAIR *looks at* STUDENT.] What time did you get home last night?

AU PAIR: Very late. Four. I came in thinking I am maybe in trouble if I am heard. But taking off shoes and creeping up stairs I am making no noise.

STUDENT: Yet you still managed to get up this morning.

AU PAIR: Oh yes. I get Tom up, ready for kindergarten, and make him breakfast, get him off, oh yes, no one can say Heidi doesn't do her job.

STUDENT: Did anyone call?

AU PAIR: On the phone? No, no calls this morning.

STUDENT: I don't mean on the phone, I mean, did any one call here? I'm expecting someone. You know him, my mate Robbie.

AU PAIR: Your friend with the beard.

STUDENT: Yeah, and the hideous ponytail. Has he come here? Have I missed him? Did he ring the bell?

AU PAIR: No, he hasn't been.

STUDENT: Four o'clock you say you came home. You know what that makes you? A dirty stop-out.

AU PAIR: I'm not dirty.

STUDENT: So where exactly did you go, where you had so much fun you couldn't tear yourself away till the wee small hours?

AU PAIR: I should know. I know it's very bad of me but I don't. A club. Over on the west somewhere.

STUDENT: Where the rough people are.

AU PAIR: No, I am meeting some very nice people, actually, over there. Not rough. Charming, polite, interesting, serious, very committed. Girls I am meeting first in bar, Sharon, Kelly, Debbie, then later in club I am meeting man.

STUDENT: Meeting man. I love it. That means making the beast with two backs, right? [AU PAIR *blushes.*]

AU PAIR: No, nothing like that. It was conversation.

STUDENT: Meeting man means conversation. I don't think so.

AU PAIR: I am actually writing now to him, continuing dialogue.

STUDENT: Nobody writes letters any more.

AU PAIR: I do. I'm old-fashioned.

STUDENT: I'm very hot, are you?

AU PAIR: No. I'm feeling quite cool, thank you.

STUDENT: Oh. I'd like a glass of water. Will you bring me a glass of water? Please? A long glass of cold water. I would regard it as a great honour if you would. [AU PAIR *takes glass from the cupboard and goes to the sink.*] Be sure to let the tap run. I want a nice cool glass of water.

[AU PAIR *stands with her back to* STUDENT *at the sink. The tap runs.* STUDENT *reads the letter.* AU PAIR *turns and hands* STUDENT *the glass of water. He drinks the glass. He sets the glass on the table.*]

STUDENT: How was my father this morning?

AU PAIR: He seemed actually, he wasn't very...

STUDENT: Friendly?

AU PAIR: No. He's always friendly. He was just well, you know ...

STUDENT: No, I don't know. You've got to spell it out. Be explicit.

AU PAIR: He seemed ...

STUDENT: Hungover? Stoned? Hey man ...

AU PAIR: Subdued. He said he had big ... review ... in court.

STUDENT: Oh yes, right enough. He's got a fucking nightmare on today.

AU PAIR: What is this exactly?

STUDENT: Oh, exactly.

AU PAIR: A big trial?

STUDENT: No, just a little application for leave to apply for a judicial review.

AU PAIR: What is this?

STUDENT: Another opportunity for lawyers to make more money. [AU PAIR *still does not understand.*] The prisoners are out, right? But the ones who escaped, years back, if they come north, they go to jail. So, they ... well, their party, they want to take the Secretary of State to court to make him let them come home. But they can't do that unless daddy says they can. Which hopefully he won't. These prisoners haven't done their whack so why should they get the amnesty? The whole thing's a bloody try on. But there you go, that's the legal system for you. It's a joke.

AU PAIR: Why study law then when you're going to end up in this world?

STUDENT: God I hate you. You're so much more intelligent than me.

AU PAIR: So, tell me, why?

STUDENT: It's a dirty job, Heidi, but someone has to do it.

AU PAIR: You're a cynic.

STUDENT: I saw you in the shower. I stood and watched, for a long time. And you knew I was there, didn't you?

AU PAIR: You want to do good but you fear the world will make you do bad. You have a dilemma.

STUDENT: That's a big word. Where did you get it?

AU PAIR: In my dictionary.

[*She gestures at the dictionary on table.*]

STUDENT: What's your man called?

AU PAIR: Who?

STUDENT: Lover boy here, the one you're writing to.

AU PAIR: His real name is Frank Milligan but some call him Ten Rounds.

STUDENT: He's famous you know. Here.

AU PAIR: I wouldn't know.

STUDENT: Has he fallen for you? Are you in love?

AU PAIR: It was not like that.

STUDENT: Go on, what was it like? Tell me. You can trust me—I'm a romantic.

AU PAIR: He is man in deep trouble, I think. Very committed. Big part in the struggle.

STUDENT: Oh, big hero.

AU PAIR: Very complex.

STUDENT: Uh-huh.

AU PAIR: Strong smell of farm ... but not cows ... more ... chemical ... fertiliser. We have big factory making in Nürnberg.

STUDENT: So you slept with him then?

AU PAIR: No.

STUDENT: Sorry darling, knowing how he smells is a bit of a give away.

AU PAIR: I didn't.

STUDENT: I bet he got your knickers off by talking hard. Hint, hint, I'm a republican. Now uncross your legs. Oh good on you girl, I'm coming in. It's our most popular seduction technique.

AU PAIR: Alban, you're wrong. It's not true what you're saying.

STUDENT: If I got a pound for every time a man on the pull said he was in the Irish Republican Army, I'd be a millionaire several times over.

AU PAIR: I am modern but I am not easy.

STUDENT: Oh, talk some more like that.

AU PAIR: I am not like you say.

STUDENT: I love it when you're red and roused.

AU PAIR: I make decisions for sensible reasons not because like you say I'm impressed.

STUDENT: Of course you don't. I don't know what I was saying. [*He strokes her cheek.*] I don't think we should pretend. I think we should bow to the inevitable. I think I should be one of your sensible decisions, don't you?

AU PAIR: What happens if Robbie is coming and rings bell?

STUDENT: We let it ring. We don't have to answer the door.

AU PAIR: Yes, it's possible.

STUDENT: Have you decided?

AU PAIR: Now I am hot. I am thirsty.

STUDENT: Is it my turn to get you a glass of water?

AU PAIR: I am thinking, it would be nice.

STUDENT: Will you have it out of my glass? [*She nods. He takes the glass to the sink and runs the tap. She puts her letter and her dictionary in a drawer. He returns. He gives the glass to* AU PAIR. *She drinks greedily. As she drinks, he pulls her blouse free around her waist. She finishes the glass. He takes it and puts it on the table.*] Do you know what I think? [*She closes her eyes and offers her face. He takes her glasses off.*] The decision made for sensible reasons is one you never regret ...

[*She lies back on the table. The glass falls and smashes.*]

***

STUDENT *goes round the kitchen sweeping glass fragments into little piles.* AU PAIR *follows with the dustpan and brush and sweeps them up.*

STUDENT: Excuse me, I am thinking you missed a bit there.

[*He impersonates her accent well.* AU PAIR *laughs as she sweeps the shards she missed.*]

AU PAIR: We miss piece and Tom cuts his foot and it won't be so easy to explain, what? [*She does a bad impersonation of a Northern Irish accent.*] Oh, he's cutting his foot on a bit of glass, did he? And how did the glass breaking? You knocked it off the table, Heidi. And how are you knocking the glass off the table, Heidi? Oh, Heidi, but I thought you were a nice au pair.

STUDENT [*replies in a German accent*]: Oh but I am, Mrs. Jameson, but I am, I am very respectable girl. My mother would be proud of me.

AU PAIR [*speaks in her own voice*]: Maybe, on second thoughts, I'm thinking—maybe she'd say I'm—[*The doorbell rings.*] I will get it, shall I?

STUDENT: No, it's all right. I will. That'll be my mate, Robbie. [*He goes out. Voices off stage. He returns.*] Yes, we'll go far in the world. As predicted, that's my mate Robbie. [*He moves off again.*] Tell dad and the second Mrs. Jameson I'll be in for me grub later.

AU PAIR: Don't rush off. I'm thinking it is time for coffee. Or tea.

I thinking now I'm in Ireland long enough, I can stew tea like the best of them. Bring your friend in. I don't have to go for Tom for another half an hour.

STUDENT: No, we're off to the park. When it's hot, like today, girls take a lot of their clothes off, and Robbie, he likes to look. It's the only opportunity he gets. No girl will come near him with that horrible beard and terrible ponytail. Auf Wiedersehen, pet.

AU PAIR: Goodbye. [*He leaves.* AU PAIR *sits at the table. She gets out the letter and the dictionary. She resumes writing.*] ... a very unique connection. I am wishing to see you again. May we meet? Give me an address. I will take a taxi. It is better, I think, not to come here.

4 THE STUDENT AND THE WIFE

A student room in a student house. A very large bed. Sound of lavatory flushing and doorbell pealing. STUDENT *enters and throws himself on bed, then realises he's lying on something. He pulls out a pair of handcuffs. He hides these quickly under a pillow.* WIFE *enters wearing pashmina over her head. She carries a basket.*

STUDENT: My God, it's a shawlie.

WIFE: Who was that at the door downstairs?

STUDENT: That'll be my mate, Robbie. He's pretty disgusting, isn't he?

WIFE: Do you think he recognised me?

STUDENT: No.

WIFE: Are you sure?

STUDENT: Why would he recognise you? He doesn't know who you are.

WIFE: But you promised.

STUDENT: Yeah, that I'd be here, and I am.

WIFE: No, you said I needn't worry. You said you'd open the door and bring me up and nobody'd see me.

STUDENT: Yeah but I was busy when the bell went.

WIFE: You should have been downstairs.

STUDENT: I was having a piss upstairs.

WIFE: Please, do you have to talk like that? We're not in the union bar.

STUDENT: Oh, touchy.

WIFE: No, I'm not.

STUDENT: You are.

WIFE: I should never have come. I've made a mistake.

STUDENT: You were the one who wanted to come. Now you change your mind. Once you make a decision, you should learn to stick to it.

WIFE: Let's not squabble. I can't stay long.

STUDENT: Why not?

WIFE: You know why. I'm meant to be at home.

STUDENT: What exactly does 'I can't stay long' mean?

WIFE: What it sounds like.

STUDENT: Well how long are you staying? Five minutes?

WIFE: Maybe.

STUDENT: Ten?

WIFE: I could. I don't know. I haven't decided.

STUDENT: Well, don't lurk in the doorway. Come in properly, come on.

WIFE: All right, but I'm not staying.

STUDENT: I understand. [*She steps forward. She puts her straw bag down.*] Take that thing off your head, anyway.

WIFE: It's not a thing. It's a pashmina.

STUDENT: You must be boiling.

[*He takes it off and throws it on the bed.*]

WIFE: How do you feel about me?

STUDENT: Truthfully and candidly? [*He puts his hands on her breasts.*] My God, I'm sorry but I can't stop myself.

WIFE: I don't want to be rushed.

STUDENT: God, if only you were wearing your uniform and you spoke to me like that. It would be incredibly, wonderfully, horrifyingly sexy.

WIFE: I don't wear a uniform.

STUDENT: You don't.

WIFE: No.

STUDENT: What do you wear?

WIFE: This, what I'm in now. In fact, you saw me in this dress in the office.

STUDENT: Did I?

WIFE: You said it suited me.

STUDENT: Really?

WIFE: Do you notice anything?

STUDENT: When I'm in the grip of lust, I'm afraid, no. As I expand the world shrinks.

WIFE: My hair?

STUDENT: No. No. Yes. Yes. It's changed. It's lovely.

WIFE: God, this room's stifling!

STUDENT: Well, take this off.

[*He pulls her cardigan off.*]

WIFE: I meant what I said. I don't want to be rushed.

STUDENT: But I'm all fired up.

WIFE: That's it, I'm off.

STUDENT: But it hasn't even been a minute.

WIFE: What time is it?

[*He looks at his watch.*]

STUDENT: Six-fifteen.

WIFE: I should be at my sister's. I said I was going over to see her.

STUDENT: Well, you're not. You're somewhere nicer.

[*He embraces her.*]

WIFE: Why didn't you answer my question?

STUDENT: What question?

WIFE: How do you feel about me?

STUDENT: The answer to that is that if I don't have you, now, I'm going to explode. And I'm happy with any space as long as it's wet and female. In your mouth or up either passage.

[*She separates from him.*]

WIFE: I'm too old for a couple of fumbles and goodnight, Irene. And too tired.

STUDENT: What are you talking about? I'm serious.

WIFE: Are you? Prove it to me.

STUDENT: Oh all right. Look, you're very hot. Let me help you.

[*He starts to unbutton her.*]

WIFE: That's not telling me anything. [*She stops him.*]

STUDENT: Isn't it?

WIFE: No.

STUDENT: So what do you want me to tell you? I love you.

WIFE: How many others have you said that to?

STUDENT: No one.

WIFE: You must have.

STUDENT: No. Only you. At the moment.

WIFE: I was going to ring and cancel this, you know. I actually wrote out what I wanted to say, got my mobile, got your number up, but I just couldn't punch the little button to dial through. I am pathetic. Anyway, that's it. I will go.

STUDENT: You make me so happy. Or you could.

[*He kisses her. She returns his kiss, then backs away.*]

WIFE: What am I doing?

STUDENT: This has got to be better than sneaking out from the Higgins' party and going into the bushes. What if someone had come out and caught us? Here's safe. That was risky.

WIFE: I don't want to think about it, if you don't mind,

STUDENT: And I had to talk to your husband after. Now that was freaky.

WIFE: Didn't you hear? Don't talk about it.

STUDENT: I want to do it again only more comfortably.

WIFE: Have you got anything to drink?

STUDENT: Yeah.

[*He gets a bottle of wine and two glasses from behind the bed.*]

WIFE: Have you ever had anyone else in here? [*He pours.*] No, actually, don't answer that question. It was a stupid question to ask. [*She takes glass, empties it, and holds glass out for a refill. He refills it.*] Sometimes one asks questions. You get an answer. You think, that's fine, I can cope with that. And then bang, you wake up at four a.m. and guess what? [*She empties the glass.*] You can't. [*She holds the glass out again.*] Three and that's it.

STUDENT: And what, you're anyone's? [*He pours.*]

WIFE: No. [*She empties glass.*] I can hold my drink. And just to show you I'll have a fourth if you don't mind.

[*He pours. She drinks.*]

STUDENT: If you want to go home now that's fine.

[*He pours her fifth glass.*]

WIFE: I probably will when I've finished this.

[*She empties glass.*]

STUDENT: But before that there's something I want you to know.

WIFE: Which is?

STUDENT: I know you are unhappy. And I want to make you happy.

WIFE: Do you? [*The bottle is empty. She takes his glass, sips it, and then offers him a sip.*] Do you? Do you mean that?
[*He throws the bottle on the bed. She's got both hands full. He starts to kiss her.*]

STUDENT: I have been thinking about you, this, and nothing else for days. I am going to explode, I swear. Please, please help me. [*She empties the second glass, throws both glasses on the bed.*] Just put those magic hands down there, please, and we'll talk later.
[*She slips a hand behind his belt.*]

***

STUDENT: Oh my God. Oh, I'm so sorry.

WIFE: Have you got a hanky?

STUDENT: There might be a tissue in my pocket, I think.
[WIFE *pulls her wet hand free. With the other hand she feels his pocket.*]

WIFE: No, you haven't. But I think I've got some. [*She sniffs her hand.*] Smells of sawdust and fishbones. [*She sits on bed and reaches for basket.*] I'm in luck. [*She fishes out a tissue and wipes her wet hand.*]

STUDENT: I was over-excited.

WIFE: Yes, well I wouldn't worry about it.

STUDENT: Oh God, I'm an embarrassment.

WIFE: It happens.

STUDENT: I'm an utter drivelling idiot.

WIFE: Don't worry.
[*He removes the glasses and the bottle from the bed and puts them away behind the bed.*]

STUDENT: Has it ever happened to you before?

WIFE: Me personally?

STUDENT: No, it couldn't happen to you, Emma, you're a woman. I meant were you ever with a man it's happened to? When he was with you?

WIFE: Let me think? [*She thinks.*] No, never.

STUDENT: Ouch. I'm your first, am I?
[*He sits beside her. She smoothes her hair and eyebrows.*]

WIFE: I said not to worry.

STUDENT: Robbie, myself and a few other mates, were having a few shandies last week and the conversation got onto our most embarrassing experiences. At the start it was all buying condoms from the chemist and you're sixteen, and the assistant's a young girl who asks you to repeat what you want three times and that sort of crack. Then Robbie said we was all good friends, we had to talk about the really excruciating stuff. And you know what? With every one of us it was the same. It was getting into bed and going off like I did before anything happened.

WIFE: Really. And some of us don't even get into bed, do we? Or even get our clothes off. One touch ... boom! kepow!

[*They laugh together. She laughs louder than he does.*]

STUDENT: You know what's marvellous? I can talk to you like my mates.

WIFE: Really?

STUDENT: Abso-bloody-lutely. It means this is right. This is the real thing. It's not just lust. It's a relationship.

WIFE: Do you love me?

STUDENT: Yes.

WIFE: I'm a bit tipsy.

STUDENT: I hardly had a sip.

WIFE: I'm happy, relaxed, and hopefully you're happy and unrelaxed. Aren't those supposed to be the perfect conditions? The man sober, the woman not so sober.

STUDENT: Just stand up, would you?

WIFE: Why?

STUDENT: Just do as I tell you for once.

WIFE: Oh all right.

[*She stands.* STUDENT *whips the duvet off the bed.*]

STUDENT: Now lie back. [*She flops back.*] Shoes. [*She kicks her shoes off.*]

WIFE: I've only got five minutes.

STUDENT: What, you think this'll take any longer? [*He throws the duvet over his shoulders like a cape.*] Now put your arms over your head.

WIFE: Why? Are you going to restrain me?

STUDENT: I don't want those magic hands down below. [*She puts her hands over her head.*] Plus, for you no guilt. You can say I did it all. Now hold on, I'm coming in.

[*He jumps on top of her, covering them both with the duvet.*]

***

STUDENT *and* WIFE *are in bed under the duvet.*

WIFE: I really should go.

STUDENT: Not yet.

WIFE: Do you want me to be in trouble? [*Her head pops out from the bottom of the bed.*] What time is it? [*His head pops out of the top. He shows her the watch on his wrist.*] Oh, my God! I must go. [*She jumps out of bed, clothes in disarray. The handcuffs are on.*] Here. Take these off. I am in such trouble, oh my God, oh my God. [*He takes them off. She begins to dress.*] Find my shoes will you? [*He jumps out of bed, also in disarray. He dresses and begins to search.*] What am I going to say? I was only meant to be gone an hour. [*He locates her shoes.*] Why didn't you notice the time?

STUDENT: Dunno.

WIFE [*stepping into her shoes*]: Well don't slip up like that again in future. Oh my God. What will I say?

STUDENT: I thought you were supposed to be at your sisters.

WIFE: You're a terrible liar. I couldn't have been there this long.

STUDENT: Well, let's hope you're a good one then.

[*She takes a make-up bag and a hairbrush from her basket.*]

WIFE: Let's see. Never went to sister's. Bumped into friend, had coffee, then to Forestside. Mammoth shop. Everything through the till, everything bagged up, then I discovered, no card, no chequebook, nothing. Shopping aborted, horrible realisation, menopause had come early.

STUDENT: That's pathetic.

WIFE: You'll find in life the worse the marriage the stupider the excuses.

[*She begins to make her face up. She continues throughout the exchange that follows.*]

STUDENT: How's the world of low-level intelligence gathering?

WIFE: Fine.

STUDENT: Now ask me.

WIFE: Why? You're coming in next Tuesday. You can tell me about your disgusting fellow students and collect your money then.

STUDENT: This can't wait.

WIFE: Of course it can.

STUDENT: It's not about the uni.

WIFE: All right, how's your world of low-level surveillance?

STUDENT: Funny you should ask. Let me give you a name. Ten Rounds Milligan.

WIFE: Yeah—and your point is?

STUDENT: Well, Heidi ...

WIFE: Heidi? Not a girlfriend I hope?

STUDENT: The au pair, at home.

WIFE: I'm not up to speed on your parents' domestic arrangements.

STUDENT: Come round, I'll introduce you to everyone.

WIFE: Don't be stupid. What would your father say?

STUDENT: He'd say I got lucky.

WIFE: I don't know what I'm doing with you. If my husband ...

STUDENT: Our Heidi and Ten are an item.

WIFE: What's wrong with that? They're consenting adults.

STUDENT: And he stinks. Of fertiliser. We know what that means.

WIFE: Heidi told you this?

STUDENT: Yes.

WIFE: My guess, if she told you, is that you're sleeping with her. Please tell me I'm wrong.

STUDENT: You're wrong.

WIFE: Why don't I believe you?

STUDENT: I think you should have a word. I think someone should look at our friend.

WIFE: We have too much to do and not enough Indians to do it. Give me one good reason other than what this ... friend ... Heidi says.

STUDENT: Not a friend. Employee.

WIFE: Whatever.

STUDENT: Isn't that enough—what she said?

WIFE: No, it isn't. He's on licence. His lot is on ceasefire.

STUDENT: Yes, but he has friends who aren't.

WIFE: You know your trouble? You're getting above yourself. You're forgetting who you are.

STUDENT: I'm not.

WIFE: You are.

STUDENT: All right, I am. Feel better? Now what are you going to do?

WIFE: It is like I said. Too big for your boots. Alban, this conversation is now concluded.

STUDENT: I won't shut up and fuck off. You must do something.

WIFE: Stick to what you do best. Come in, tell me what's going on in the uni, take your pounds, go home. Leave the rest to those who know.

STUDENT: You know what this makes you?

WIFE: I'm sure you'll tell me.

STUDENT: Actually I can't be bothered.

WIFE: Oh go on, tell me.

STUDENT: No.

WIFE: Tell me.

STUDENT: An idiot.

WIFE: Amazing—attractive young man like you should screw idiots.

STUDENT: I meant you're idiotic.

WIFE: I don't think so.

STUDENT: You're twisting everything round.

WIFE: You said it. I heard it.

STUDENT: I said it. I didn't mean it. Of course you're not an idiot.

WIFE: No? Isn't that what you really think?

STUDENT: I meant you were idiotic. You know that.

WIFE: No, first I was an idiot. Then you qualified.

STUDENT: I didn't mean you were an idiot.

WIFE: I've hurt your feelings, obviously. I'm sorry. Maybe this idiot should throw in an extra tenner next Tuesday? Or maybe twenty? Would that make up for not being taken seriously?

STUDENT: It's nothing to do with that.

WIFE: Exactly. You said it because actually that's what you really think, don't you?

STUDENT: No.

WIFE: And next time you have a few shandies with Robbie and your mates you'll steer the conversation to older women you've shagged and you'll talk about this idiot, won't you?

STUDENT: I won't.

WIFE: Why wouldn't you? You went through all the women you came too quickly with. And now I'm on that list. So why wouldn't I be on the list of old slags you've had?

STUDENT: You've got everything wrong.

WIFE: Alban, the damage is done. Don't make it worse by making out you never said it.

STUDENT: I meant your attitude is idiotic.

WIFE: Once a word is out in the world, you can't take it back. There's nothing more to be said. But I'm grateful. You should always know where you stand and at least this idiot now knows where she stands. So thank you. Thank you very much. [*She grabs her things and hurries towards the door.*] If I meet Robbie on the stairs I'll scream.

STUDENT: No, he's gone to judo tonight. [*She hurries out. He shakes his head and laughs.*] My God, she's absolutely barking mad.

5 THE WIFE AND THE HUSBAND

WIFE *lies in bed reading* The Lady with the Dog & Other Stories *by Anton Chekhov.* HUSBAND *comes in through the door and closes it behind him. He is in a bathrobe. She looks up.*

WIFE: You said you were coming straight up. What were you doing?

HUSBAND: Writing.

WIFE: Couldn't it have waited?

HUSBAND: No.

WIFE: What were you writing about?

HUSBAND: Politics, the peace process, the usual old nonsense.

WIFE: Then it could have waited if it was the usual old nonsense.

HUSBAND: Is this the menopause?

WIFE: No.

HUSBAND: Then what is going on? I'm hardly through the door and you're having a go.

WIFE: I'm not.

HUSBAND: Really? You could have fooled me.

WIFE: You said you were coming up.

HUSBAND: And I have. I'm here, aren't I?

WIFE: One hour later.

HUSBAND: I never said I was coming immediately.

WIFE: Oh I'm sorry, I thought that was the meaning of 'I'll be right up.'

HUSBAND: I meant, as you well know, I'll be up when I finish.

WIFE: Don't slither out of it. We both know what it means.

HUSBAND: Anyway, you saw me writing. You know I can't stop midflow.

WIFE: Why not?

HUSBAND: Why should I? If I came out to your work and said, right, stop now, you wouldn't. You'd say go away. But because I happen to work at home you think you can tell me what to do. Well, sorry, you can't.

WIFE: You could have done it tomorrow and come an hour ago.

HUSBAND: If there's something good, you have to spoil it, don't you? Yes, I was too long. But as I was writing I suddenly thought, this is ridiculous—she's there, I'm here, and we haven't seen each other lately. I came up filled with good feelings, but you couldn't let me show those—oh no. I wish I'd stayed at my desk now. I wouldn't have got my head bitten off.

WIFE: Well, that's just what I need at the end of an awful day. Thank you. [*She resumes reading.*]

HUSBAND: Ah, another successful evening. All right, go on, tell me what happened?

WIFE: Nothing much. I've just been made to look like an idiot, that's all.

HUSBAND: So what did you do?

WIFE: How did I act the idiot? Why do you assume it's my fault?

HUSBAND: Don't react to my question. Just tell me what happened.

WIFE: What happened? I ... ah ...

HUSBAND: I'm waiting with bated breath for this.

[*She looks up from her book.*]

WIFE: I got told something. Some people looked into it. They couldn't find anything. Then today I was hauled in about it and my knuckles were rapped. [*She resumes reading her book.*]

HUSBAND: I'm afraid that wasn't terribly illuminating. Let's start again. Tell me what happened. In concrete terms.

WIFE: I shouldn't.

HUSBAND: I know you shouldn't, but sometimes shouldn't doesn't apply. What do you want? Do you want to feel less rotten? Or do you want to wallow in your misery?

WIFE: Of course I don't.

HUSBAND: Then tell me what's the matter.

[*She looks up from her book.*]

WIFE: You won't discuss it with anyone, will you?

HUSBAND: Never. It'll stay within these four walls.

WIFE: Ten Rounds Milligan ...

HUSBAND: Ah ... he's one of my favourites.

WIFE: I was told he's making a bomb. A big one.

HUSBAND: Oh God, really?

WIFE: Allegedly. I reported this. Checks were made. Nothing showed. Then today I'm told my lies could destroy everything that had been achieved over the last few years and I'm an enemy of the Agreement and I'm to shut up.

HUSBAND: The bastards.

WIFE: You won't go back to the paper with this?

HUSBAND: Why would I?—you said it wasn't true.

WIFE: Even one telephone call could finish me.

HUSBAND: I said, didn't I? If you don't trust me don't tell me things. You do, trust me, don't you? [*She shrugs.*] Oh lovely.

WIFE: No, I'm just being paranoid. Your paper wouldn't—of course not. I've nothing to worry about.

HUSBAND: Meaning what exactly?

WIFE: You know.

HUSBAND: I don't.

WIFE: They, your paper ...

HUSBAND: Yes.

WIFE: They support the agreement. Why go into something that would make them look stupid?

HUSBAND: Because they're a paper, actually. That's what papers do.

WIFE: Yeah, but not yours. They've got their line and they stick to it. They want this to be a nice wee place where we all make jam and get on and never a bad word is said.

HUSBAND: Come off it.

WIFE: It's true. It's not ...

HUSBAND: It's not a what?

WIFE: Not a proper newspaper.

HUSBAND: So what does that make me? Not a proper journalist?

WIFE: I didn't say ...

HUSBAND: Ah, ah, ah.

[*She resumes reading.*]

WIFE: You never noticed my hair did you?

HUSBAND: Is that why you're in a fury?

WIFE: No.

HUSBAND: Well, what's that to do with anything then?

WIFE: It's been dyed and cut a week and not one word have you said.

HUSBAND: I thought you were pissed off because I didn't come to bed. Or because I work for a crap paper. But no, sorry, it's your bloody hair.

WIFE: And your point is?

HUSBAND: Well, what's this with the hair suddenly? Can we please stick to one grievance at a time? I don't deal with multi-grievance situations. They're too confusing.

WIFE: Well, you should learn.

HUSBAND: Oh, should I?

WIFE: Everything is connected. In life you never get one thing at a time. It always comes together.

HUSBAND: Oh, I get it. I kept you waiting. I work for appeasers. I didn't notice your bloody hair. Come on—what else? Let's get them all out. Then we can have the mother of all rows. Come on.

WIFE: I don't want a row. I hate rows.

HUSBAND: Oh really. So—what? You're just making conversation?

WIFE: I don't want a row.

HUSBAND: So why did you start the moment I came in through the door?

WIFE: You said you'd come up an hour ago. You didn't. That's the story of our marriage. I'm waiting and you're writing. And I'm fed up with it. That's what I'm saying. Please, don't do this any more. That's all.

HUSBAND: So don't be a journalist, you mean?

WIFE: I didn't say that.

HUSBAND: But that is what you mean.

WIFE: No.

HUSBAND: Yes. If I didn't write this wouldn't happen. Therefore stop doing it.

WIFE: Just organise yourself better. You spend more time with your computer than me.

HUSBAND: Oh don't start, 'He loves his keyboard more than me.'

WIFE: But you do.

HUSBAND: You want me to be someone else, don't you? Well, Emma, no can do. If I don't suit, tough, let's go our separate ways.

WIFE: That's always the way with you, isn't it?

HUSBAND: What is 'always the way'?

WIFE: Every time I criticise, you go, right, let's get a divorce. Well, fine—that's what you want, let's do it. Let's go to a solicitor. Tomorrow. We can sell the house ... buy two flats. Come on, what are we waiting for? Let's do it.

HUSBAND: You know that isn't what I want or meant.

WIFE: So why did you bring it up then?

HUSBAND: This is stupid.

WIFE: Why did you bring it up?

HUSBAND: Because it was in response to you wanting me to cease being a writer and become someone else.

[*She starts reading again.*]

WIFE: That isn't what I want.

HUSBAND: What do you want?

WIFE: Nothing. [*She turns a page.*] I just had a rotten day that's all.

HUSBAND: You had a rotten day?

WIFE: Yes, actually.

[*He goes to her side of the bed.*]

HUSBAND: Here, let's put the book away, shall we?

[*With his left hand he goes to take the book.*]

WIFE: Why have you moved your ring?

[*He glances at his left hand.*]

HUSBAND: My knuckles swell up in the heat. And when I'm typing and it's tight, it hurts. [*He swaps his wedding ring from his little to his ring finger.*] My fanny magnet. Not. [*He takes the book.*] You'll ruin your eyes reading in this light, you know. [*He looks at the book.*] *The Lady with the Dog and Other Stories*—Anton Chekhov.

WIFE: Next month's book club.

HUSBAND: Know the name, never read any. Any good?

WIFE: Sad.

HUSBAND: Oh.

WIFE: No, sad is good.

HUSBAND: The title story then—what's it about?

WIFE: A serial adulterer falls for a mousy married woman.

HUSBAND: But there's a twist? She rejects him?

WIFE: No. She loves him and he loves her right back.

HUSBAND: I hope this isn't giving you ideas?

WIFE: Can I tell you my theory?

HUSBAND: Don't let me stop you.

WIFE: I bet there was more hanky-panky in the past.

HUSBAND: What, than nowadays?

WIFE: Marriages were contracts then. For love you had to go outside the home. *Ergo*, more infidelity.

HUSBAND: Oh, that makes me feel much better. We'll stay solid because you know I love you.

WIFE: When you say it I do. But at other times you don't so I forget.

HUSBAND: But sometimes you have to ...

WIFE: What?

HUSBAND: Pull back.

WIFE: Why?

HUSBAND: You have to pace yourself.

WIFE: You do?

HUSBAND: Yes ... and think of the advantages.

WIFE: None spring to my mind. What are they?

HUSBAND: Look at us. This hasn't been one dull marriage end to end, has it? Sometimes we're in love. Then we're just friends. Then we're in love again. Now just imagine if things had gone on as they were when we started?

WIFE: I wouldn't have minded.

HUSBAND: I'd be dead. Can I get in?

WIFE: I'm not stopping you.

[*He gets into the bed.*]

HUSBAND: I remember thinking back then, let's just be friends for a bit. Here, put your head on my shoulder. We can be lovers again later. And it worked.

WIFE: Because each time we have another honeymoon?

HUSBAND: Aye.

WIFE: Where are we in the cycle?

HUSBAND: Start of another honeymoon. I'll scratch your back if you want.

WIFE: Goody. [*She snuggles down, turning her back to him.*] Could it be like the start all the time if I were different?

HUSBAND: No. Anyway, I wouldn't want you different. Take your thing off.

WIFE: Careful with your nails, Mr. Wolf.

[*She kicks her nightdress out from the end of the bed. He scratches her back under the covers during the exchange.*]

HUSBAND: Do you feel better now your troubles are off your chest?

WIFE: Yes.

HUSBAND: That doesn't sound like a convincing yes.

WIFE: How's this? Yes.

HUSBAND: How does your back feel?

WIFE: Lovely.

HUSBAND: Do you want to go straight to sleep?

WIFE: No.

HUSBAND: Do you want to do it with the light on or off?

WIFE: I don't mind.

HUSBAND: Let's be old-fashioned. Let's have the light off, shall we? [*He turns off the light. He kisses her. Initially she returns his kisses, then she stops.*] I have the feeling ... is something the matter?

WIFE: No ...

HUSBAND: Are you sure?

WIFE: Well.

HUSBAND: I thought you were on?

WIFE: I was.

HUSBAND: Why don't you just lie back and let me ...

WIFE: The thing is I'm a bit sore at the moment. It might be thrush. It'd be safer to leave it, I think.

HUSBAND: Thrush, oh God, no, we don't want that. Suck me off then?

WIFE: I don't know. No, I'm too tired.

HUSBAND: Hand-job?

WIFE: No, DIY if you're horny. Otherwise, let's go to sleep, honey.

HUSBAND: Oh all right, I'm not that desperate. Spoons or back-to-back?

WIFE: Spoons.

[*She turns her back. He nestles against her.*]

HUSBAND: Jesus, imagine if what you said about Ten Rounds Milligan was true?

WIFE: It isn't.

HUSBAND: But what if it was? That would be it, wouldn't it? It would be back to war.

WIFE: But it isn't.

HUSBAND: You don't know it isn't. You've just been told it isn't. I bet someone, somewhere has taken the decision not to go into him because it'll cause too much trouble.

WIFE: We agreed, our conversation stays here.

HUSBAND: But couldn't I just ...

WIFE: No. You can't make inquiries or anything. You promised.

HUSBAND: What would the harm be?

WIFE: You poke about and word gets back—and it will—I'm dead, that's what.

HUSBAND: All right, don't worry.

WIFE: And I mean it. You can't go to someone else and get them to do it either.

HUSBAND: Of course not.

WIFE: You can't go back on your word. That's final.

HUSBAND: I said I won't and I won't.

WIFE: Fine.

HUSBAND: Goodnight, Mrs. Wife.

WIFE: Goodnight, Mr. Husband.

6 THE HUSBAND AND THE PR GIRL

The hospitality suite of a hotel. A very big sofa. HUSBAND *sits at one end smoking a cigar.* PR GIRL *in a sash sits at the other. She is finishing a knickerbocker glory out of glass with a stem.*

HUSBAND: How is it?

PR GIRL: Lovely, thank you.

HUSBAND: I could get you another. Room service will oblige.

PR GIRL: This is my second. One more and I'll explode.

HUSBAND: Have a top up.

[*He fills her wine glass.*]

PR GIRL: I don't think I should.

HUSBAND: Ah, go on. One'll not hurt.

PR GIRL: No, one won't but I've already had a few.

[*He examines the bottle.*]

HUSBAND: Look, it's not even half-empty.

PR GIRL: That's our second though.

HUSBAND: Oh, I forgot.

PR GIRL: Anyone'd think you want me off my face.

HUSBAND: Why would I want that?

PR GIRL: You might be a rogue.

HUSBAND: Don't be silly. I'm a man of probity.

PR GIRL: What does that mean?

HUSBAND: I'm a gentleman.

PR GIRL: Fair enough.

HUSBAND: Do you do this all the time?

PR GIRL: Take ice creams from strange men?

HUSBAND: No, this sort of gig?

PR GIRL: This is the first I've done for—I've forgotten what they're called. Must be the wine. [*She squints down at the sash.*] Fitzer's Irish Spa Water. [*She pulls the sash off and reads.*] The choice of the Irish for centuries. Water you can trust.

[*She goes to put the sash back on.*]

HUSBAND: Leave it off.

PR GIRL: Why?

HUSBAND: I want to look at you. Not the representative of Irish water you can trust.

PR GIRL: What's the time?

[*He looks at his watch.*]

HUSBAND: Just after eleven.

PR GIRL: Oh well then, I'm off the payroll.

[*The sash goes on the floor. He picks it up and looks at it.*]

HUSBAND: It's not very nice. It's made of plastic.

PR GIRL: You think that's tacky, you should see me last week.

HUSBAND: Why?

PR GIRL: Kenny's Krunchy Krisps—Triple K—do you know them?

HUSBAND: Ah ...

PR GIRL: You do. Triple K—Kenny's Krunchy Krisps—it's all in Ks.

HUSBAND: Yeah, I know them.

PR GIRL: Belfast Castle, launch of the new spicy range ... I have to dress up, as a Triple K crisp packet, and it's rubber. Ever worn rubber?

HUSBAND: I can't say I have.

PR GIRL: Don't try it at home. So here's me, completely encased, with just my head and hands and my feet free. No air going in or out. It's rubber and well you can imagine. Like a pig I was. The sweat was gushing. By the time I'd finished dishing out flyers and samples, everything underneath was wringing wet.

HUSBAND: Really.

PR GIRL: At the end of the evening, and it was a three hour gig, I stripped right off in the poxy changing room they give us and I literally had to wring my smalls out. Honest.

HUSBAND: My goodness.

PR GIRL: Then I put them back on still damp. So of course, I was shivering in the taxi. The driver, he said get in the front and he'd put the heat on. Well, when warm air meets cold wet knickers you get a funny smell. But he never said nothing. When I got back my mother was waiting. She looks after my wee man Lukey when I'm working. By now the damp had soaked out through my clothes and my mother said, 'What were you doing? Wet tee-shirts?' I said, 'Mother, I don't do that sort of thing anymore.' I did before but it was horrible. I don't think she believed me.

HUSBAND: Who's this wee man?

PR GIRL: My baby.

HUSBAND: Is there a father?

PR GIRL: Unfortunately.

HUSBAND: Oh dear. That bad. It didn't work out?

PR GIRL: I was stupid. He was reckless. But I've a bonny three-year-old to show for it, so I shouldn't complain. I look after him in the day and then at night, like Cinderella, I come out and party—if that's what you'd call this. Well, there you have it. That's my life.

HUSBAND: So you live at home?

PR GIRL: Pathetic, isn't it? My age and can't cut the apron strings. And I long to. At the same time, ma looks after Luke when I'm working. It's so hard to know what to do.

HUSBAND: It's just you and her at home, is it?

PR GIRL: And two younger sisters and a brother.

HUSBAND: Where's your father?

PR GIRL: He met someone on holiday in Spain. They live in Wigan now.

HUSBAND: I'm sorry.

PR GIRL: Maybe it was meant. He was the only Prod on the street. Life was a bit hairy sometimes. Internment night was always a nightmare.

HUSBAND: So, Cinders, do you have to be back before midnight?

PR GIRL: I can be back any time.

HUSBAND: Your mother sounds very accommodating.

PR GIRL: Yeah, she is.

HUSBAND: What would happen if you didn't go home at all?

PR GIRL: Nothing. I'm a big girl.

HUSBAND: Do you know what I'm going to do now?

PR GIRL: What?

HUSBAND: Something I've been itching to do.

PR GIRL: What?

HUSBAND: I'm going to kiss you. Can I?

[*She shrugs.*]

PR GIRL: Go on.

[*He kisses her.*]

HUSBAND: You taste of cream, you know.

PR GIRL: Well, I am sweet.

HUSBAND: How many men have you said that to?

PR GIRL: That's a daft question and I won't answer.

HUSBAND: I'd say ten.

PR GIRL: Ten!

HUSBAND: All right, twenty.

PR GIRL: Why don't you say a hundred then?

HUSBAND: God, really?

PR GIRL: Only kidding. That's my humour.

HUSBAND: All based on exaggeration, is it?

PR GIRL: I wish someone called me sweet once in a while.

HUSBAND: You are sweet, very sweet. How's that?

PR GIRL: Thank you.

HUSBAND: Surely men must be queuing up to tell you that?

PR GIRL: I wish.

HUSBAND: Well there must be one in your life, at least, who does?

PR GIRL: Well ... I don't know ... there is ... sort of ... but, no, we're going nowhere.

HUSBAND: Why?

PR GIRL: He lectures at the university and I'm ... well, I'm hardly the brain of Belfast.

HUSBAND: He must be a fool in that case. Sorry, do you mind?

PR GIRL: No.

HUSBAND: But then intellectuals often are. They fail to see the obvious. I mean, my God, you are wonderful, absolutely wonderful.

PR GIRL: You're good with words, aren't you?

HUSBAND: Not that good. Steady on.

PR GIRL: You talk very well. What do you do?

HUSBAND: I write.

PR GIRL: Of course. I don't know why I even asked.

HUSBAND: Questions are permitted and they are free as well.

PR GIRL: But I already knew, you see, without knowing. You know what I mean?

HUSBAND: No, tell me.

PR GIRL: From the way you talked to the suits and the way you came and talked to me earlier, I knew you couldn't be in sales or marketing or anything. You could only work for a paper.

HUSBAND: But I cleaned the inky stains off my fingers before I came. I emptied my pockets of paper. I washed my teeth.

PR GIRL: You're not showbiz are you?

HUSBAND: No. I'm politics but I'm covering for the business correspondent tonight—he's sick.

PR GIRL: Do you know the showbiz people?

HUSBAND: Not exactly.

PR GIRL: By sight.

HUSBAND: Oh yes. I could introduce you if you like.

PR GIRL: Could you?

HUSBAND: If it would help. I could set it up. Sure. Absolutely. A promise.

PR GIRL: That would be marvellous.

HUSBAND: Can I kiss you again?

PR GIRL: Why not? [*He kisses her.*] Will you write about this tonight?

HUSBAND: A couple of hundred words, just colour. [*He gets up.*]

PR GIRL: Where are you going?

HUSBAND: I'm going over to the door.

PR GIRL: Why?

HUSBAND: Don't we want to be private?

PR GIRL: Course.

HUSBAND: And we're in luck. [*He draws a small bolt.*] We don't want anyone coming in and spoiling our conversation.

PR GIRL: So what do you write?

HUSBAND: It's mainly long pieces, the peace process, Stormont, loyalist feuds, dissident republicans, drugs, the relationship between criminals and paramilitaries and Special Branch, you know, the usual.

PR GIRL: Isn't it boring?

HUSBAND: I hope not. I try to make it interesting.

PR GIRL: Not what you do. The subject. All our politicians do is argue like schoolchildren and the paramilitaries are all just gangsters. You want to see the ones round our way. Want for nothing, yet you never see them do a day's work. All they do is beat the shite out of wee fellas who are a bit wild. And none of them have any shame. You can put their names and pictures in the papers. You can say all about them killing and torturing, and they're delighted. Worse still, round our neighbourhood everyone reads the write-ups these boys get and they go, 'Hey, good on ye, boy. You whacked him. You tarred her. A good day's work. He's a tout. She's a tramp.' All your reporting does is leave them more impressed with themselves than they already are. Mind you, who am I to talk? I dress up as a crisp packet for a living and I'm telling you your business. Sorry, I don't know what got into me.

HUSBAND: No, there's a lot of virtue in what you say.

PR GIRL: Virtue?

HUSBAND: And you have no idea how bored I am. Suit or grunt, they've been coming out with the same old shite since forever. But I have to write it down. However, just occasionally, I think, I like this work. Not because of what I do. The days are long gone when the pen could change the world. In these mad times not doing is really the only power I have left.

PR GIRL: What do you mean?

HUSBAND: Real politics is being practised here for the first time ever, right.

PR GIRL: Yes.

HUSBAND: But with a dose of bad journalism you could kill everything.

PR GIRL: Really, how?

HUSBAND: I heard a nasty rumour. Ten Rounds Milligan ... a shit. He's often in the tabloids. I was told he was making a big bomb for some friends.

PR GIRL: Typical. At it again. I hope you're going to nail him and his mates.

HUSBAND: Hold on—just imagine if I did? The Unionists, who've no fucking balls, would run. Stormont would collapse. Now hacks are shits but we can exercise discretion. We can suppress the name of the old lady shoplifter ... or gloss over the details of a suicide ... to spare the family. Similarly, we won't print the absurd conjecture somebody on ceasefire's making a bomb for someone who isn't in order to demonstrate that though officially at peace they're really still at war, wink wink. It would destroy everything. [PR GIRL *lies back on the couch.*] Am I boring you?

PR GIRL: No, no, it's all very interesting. I'm just a bit sleepy suddenly.

HUSBAND: I should stop talking.

PR GIRL: No, talk, I like your voice.

HUSBAND: I don't want to talk any more. I'm sick of my voice.

PR GIRL: I'm not.

HUSBAND: Can I show you what I really want to do?

PR GIRL: Does it involve talking?

HUSBAND: No.

PR GIRL: Go on then.

> [*He sinks to the floor, puts his arms around* PR GIRL *and lays his head on her stomach.*]

HUSBAND: Is that nice?

PR GIRL: Yeah but don't move too much, I've had too much ice cream.

HUSBAND: You're not going to be sick?

PR GIRL: Oh no.

HUSBAND: I've locked the door.

PR GIRL: Did you?

> [*She opens her eyes. He lifts his head and looks at her.*]

HUSBAND: You know I did.

PR GIRL: Couldn't someone still come in?

HUSBAND: There's as much chance of that as a snowball not melting in hell.

PR GIRL: It's always the talkers who get me.

> [*She puts her arms out.*]

***

PR GIRL *lies on the sofa.* HUSBAND *stands some way off.*

PR GIRL: What are you doing over there? Come back here. [*He moves closer.*] No closer. Sit down. [*She moves her feet. He sits and puts his left arm along the back of the sofa. His hand is in her field of vision.*] What were you doing over there?

HUSBAND: Thinking.

PR GIRL: About me?

HUSBAND: I was.

PR GIRL: Nice thoughts?

HUSBAND: I was wondering who you are.

PR GIRL: You know that. I'm the Fitzer's Irish Spa Water girl.

HUSBAND: There's more to you than that.

PR GIRL: The same's true of you.

HUSBAND: I hope so.

[*She notices something about his hand.*]

PR GIRL: You're married, aren't you? [*She takes his left hand.*] The ring might be off but there's still a white band on your skin.

HUSBAND: What can I say? Guilty as charged. I took it off at the reception. [*He takes his wedding ring out of his pocket and slips it back on his finger.*]

PR GIRL: Do you think your wife is a cheat? I bet she is.

HUSBAND: I think I'm going to go on here.

[*He stands.*]

PR GIRL: Here's me and my big mouth—don't listen to me. I was nasty for a second but the mood's passed. That's typical of me. Pay no heed.

HUSBAND: Really? [*She tugs and he sits down again. He looks at his ring finger.*] My God, you're clever.

PR GIRL: I can't be that clever. I wouldn't be in this, would I?

[*He opens his wallet and takes out a card.*]

HUSBAND: Here, that's my mobile number. Emma never answers. [*She takes it.*] You do want to see me again?

PR GIRL: Oh yeah, and I want you to meet my mother. She's really scary. She won't like you of course.

HUSBAND: Why?

PR GIRL: Wants me married.

HUSBAND: Can't help, sorry. What about your lecturer? Can't he?

PR GIRL: No ... no, I don't think we're going anywhere.

7 THE PR GIRL AND THE ACADEMIC

A room in darkness. PR GIRL *and* ACADEMIC *enter through door.*

PR GIRL: That wasn't politics, Robert.

[*He closes the door behind him.*]

ACADEMIC: Wasn't it?

PR GIRL: No, that rally tonight was just dreary people slabbering about not going back to the bad old days.

ACADEMIC: What's wrong with that?

[*He takes a lighter from his pocket and begins to light candles.*]

PR GIRL: Well, for a start, them ones never had it bad in the first place.

ACADEMIC: Welcome to Bluebeard's lair.

PR GIRL: Can't we have the light on for once.

ACADEMIC: No.

PR GIRL: But why the candles always? You know I've not actually seen here yet. Not properly.

ACADEMIC: Electric light for work, candle flame for love.

PR GIRL: Oh right. So the place is a tip?

ACADEMIC: Lights on next time.

PR GIRL: I'll believe that when it happens. So who's Bluebeard?

ACADEMIC: A character from an opera.

[*She adopts the pose of a diva.*]

PR GIRL: Doh, re, mi, fa, so, lah, di ... Never heard of him.

ACADEMIC: Just as well. Of course, they're still entitled to voice their opinion even if it is dreary.

PR GIRL: Who? What?

ACADEMIC: The ones at the rally who you were complaining about.

PR GIRL: Oh ... them ... no they're not. If your opinion isn't worth sharing I think you should keep it to yourself. Like the poem the man read on the dead of the Troubles, that was terrible.

ACADEMIC: That was a bit off.

PR GIRL: Off! And the tears, and the croaking voice. You know what he really cared about? Not the dead—well, maybe a bit— but mostly that we knew how much he cared. And everyone else tonight was the very same. If they really want to help this place, I say, go find Ten Rounds Milligan the bombmaker. Lock him up.

ACADEMIC: What's he got to do with anything?

PR GIRL: He's making a bomb.

ACADEMIC: His lot are on ceasefire.

PR GIRL: I didn't say he'd plant it.

ACADEMIC: Meaning what?

PR GIRL: He'll give it to dissidents. That way disgruntled ones like Milligan can pretend they're hitting back and still be on ceasefire.

ACADEMIC: No.

PR GIRL: Yeah.

ACADEMIC: Rubbish.

PR GIRL: All right. Don't believe me. Maybe he isn't. Maybe it was just a yarn I heard. Do we have to have more candles?

ACADEMIC: It's very romantic. Have you told the police?

PR GIRL: Romantic! You said the same last time.

ACADEMIC: So you haven't told the police?

PR GIRL: Are you mad? My name and the word 'tout' would go up on every gable in the parish. The windows of the house'd be stove in. Or we'd be petrol bombed. I'd be stripped in the street, tied up and covered in paint—and that's if they was feeling generous. I have a son, a mother, a brother and two sisters. I wouldn't do that to them.

ACADEMIC: How do you know this?

PR GIRL: Because that's what happens.

ACADEMIC: No, I mean, how do you know what you told me?

PR GIRL: I just do. One just does. There must be others who know too.

ACADEMIC: You think the police know?

PR GIRL: Bound to. Yeah.

ACADEMIC: Well, it's news to me.

PR GIRL: And them at the rally I'd imagine.

ACADEMIC: It would definitely be news to them.

PR GIRL: But it wasn't hard to find out, Robert, and that's my point. They should get out more, seeing as they care so much—and listen. Then they might be in a position to do something.

ACADEMIC: Sometimes one doesn't want the truth. The truth is unbearable sometimes.

PR GIRL: In which case—what? More crap rallies and crap poems?

ACADEMIC: They don't harm anyone.

PR GIRL: But you don't get anywhere with that carry on. All you get is everyone thinking, 'Hey, look at me, I'm fantastic, I'm for peace.' A fire in the heart just brings smoke in the head.

[*He takes a notebook out of his pocket. He writes in it.*]

PR GIRL: What are you doing?

ACADEMIC: Writing down what you said.

PR GIRL: Well add this. Some people should be put down. Like yer man, Ten.

[*He closes notebook.*]

ACADEMIC: Look, everyone at the rally was only doing their bit in the best way they know how. They can't help being middle-class wankers any more than I can. If you're born one you just have to bear it.

PR GIRL: Oh, I know. I'm being unfair.

ACADEMIC: I went to hear what was said because it's my field. I also went because I thought, show solidarity. You were there yourself. There must have been a bit of you that thought like that too.

PR GIRL: No, I was there 'cos you asked me.

ACADEMIC: But you might have gone, mightn't you, of your own accord? And taken your son?

PR GIRL: I don't know, maybe, I might. I doubt I'd have stayed though. [*She takes a candle and walks around the room peering at the shelves.*] Every time I come I think, how many books can a man have?

ACADEMIC: I am an academic. Tools of the trade.

PR GIRL: Now, tell the truth, have you read them all?

ACADEMIC: Honestly?

PR GIRL: Yes.

ACADEMIC: No. I have a fair idea what's in each one. I've plundered most of them. But read them ... never.

PR GIRL: Hey, look, this has got your name. [*She takes a book down.*] This is you, isn't it?

ACADEMIC: Yup.

PR GIRL: *Sitting on the Fence: Conflict in Northern Ireland with special reference to the role of the churches, 1966-1986.* Catchy title. Did you sell lots?

ACADEMIC: It was so big it was made into a four-part TV series.

PR GIRL: Really?

ACADEMIC: Yeah. No, only joking.

PR GIRL: I didn't know there for a second. You might have been spoofing but then ... I can't always tell with you. So how did it do, really?

ACADEMIC: My supervising tutor read it, some external verifiers read it and a few academics read it.

PR GIRL: What's that—it can't be more than six people?

ACADEMIC: No, it was published too. Ballpark figure—two hundred readers maybe.

PR GIRL: Didn't you want more people to read it after all the work you did?

ACADEMIC: Yes, well, yes, but it served its purpose. That was my thesis. It made me a doctor. It unlocked academia. I owe my position in the politics department all to her.
[*He takes the book and kisses it.*]

PR GIRL: It's a her is it? [*The book goes back on the shelf. She kicks off her shoes and rubs each sole in turn.*] Oh, my arches took a battering tonight, Doc. I feel I walked a hundred miles.

ACADEMIC: Well sit down. Use the sofa. [*He pushes her down onto the sofa.*] Take the weight off your feet. That's what it's for. [*He swings her feet onto the sofa.*]

PR GIRL: What, reclining?

ACADEMIC: Yes.

PR GIRL: I thought they had other uses.

ACADEMIC: They can.

PR GIRL: We say 'settee' at home.

ACADEMIC: What's the big deal? It's just a word.

PR GIRL: You think I'm harsh, don't you?

ACADEMIC: No, I don't.

PR GIRL: We look at tonight's rally differently from the way you do, you know.

ACADEMIC: I understand.

PR GIRL: Do you rate me?

ACADEMIC: Of course.

PR GIRL: You're not just saying that?

ACADEMIC: No.

PR GIRL: There's more to me than quips.

ACADEMIC: I know.

PR GIRL: I gave you something. You are going to use it, aren't you. Use it to get them?

ACADEMIC: Oh don't worry, it's filed away up here. [*He taps his head.*] Knowledge is power, isn't it? Thank you.

PR GIRL: Do you know where I always go wrong?

ACADEMIC: Not in your choice of men I hope.

PR GIRL: I'm not talking about men. You've got a one-track mind. No. Footwear. I mean look at that shoe.

[*She stretches over and picks one up. He takes it.*]

ACADEMIC: What's wrong with it?

PR GIRL: It's ridiculous is what's wrong with it.

ACADEMIC: For standing maybe. But it's very decorative.

PR GIRL: What does that mean?

ACADEMIC: It's pretty.

PR GIRL: Oh, pretty.

ACADEMIC: Isn't it? Aren't they?

PR GIRL: You don't mean pretty.

ACADEMIC: I do.

PR GIRL: You mean something else.

ACADEMIC: Do I? Explain me to myself, will you?

PR GIRL: From the moment you saw these, you couldn't keep your eyes off them.

ACADEMIC: This is true.

PR GIRL: And it weren't because they were decorative.

ACADEMIC: Yes, I kept wondering—will I quaff champagne from her slipper before the day ends?

PR GIRL: You liar. I saw the cogs turning in your head. I know exactly what you were thinking and it had nothing to do with drinking.

ACADEMIC: That obvious was it?

PR GIRL: Yes.

ACADEMIC: But I didn't have my tongue hanging out.

PR GIRL: No. You kept your mouth closed.

[*He takes her foot.*]

ACADEMIC: This little piggy went to market. This little piggy stayed home. This little piggy had roast beef—and I don't want to be the little piggy who gets none.

PR GIRL: Who said anything about none?

ACADEMIC: And this little piggy cried, 'Wee! Wee! Wee!' all the way home.

[*He scratches her sole. She convulses with laughter.*]

PR GIRL: Stop it. I'm very ticklish.

[*He stops tickling her but goes on holding her leg by the heel.*]

ACADEMIC: You know I'm completely smitten with you.

PR GIRL: Really, Doctor Robert?

ACADEMIC: Really.

PR GIRL: You're not ... ?

ACADEMIC: Bullshitting you? No. I'm a lonely old academic and you're a wonderful girl.

PR GIRL: I'm not ... the sharpest knife but I have my qualities.

[*He tugs the tights where they lie over her toes and then sets her foot down.*]

ACADEMIC: Do tights always have that funny feel? [*He shudders.*]

PR GIRL: Aye, if your nails catch them.

ACADEMIC: What about otherwise?

PR GIRL: No, they're fine.

ACADEMIC: Are they ever hot?

PR GIRL: Can be.

ACADEMIC: Can they give you a rash?

PR GIRL: What do you mean?

ACADEMIC: When I played cricket at school—the heat, the flannels, the box rubbing on the crotch, by the time the match was over, my inside thigh was like strawberry jam.

PR GIRL: No, tights don't do anything like that.

ACADEMIC: Oh.

PR GIRL: They can be a bit uncomfortable though.

ACADEMIC: How?

PR GIRL: Tight. Like now. I'm bigger than when I put them on this morning. That's what this heat does to me. I swell.

ACADEMIC: Well, there's no point being uncomfortable.

PR GIRL: No, I suppose not. [*She pushes her tights down. He pulls them off and throws them into the darkness.*] Careful. Those were three ninety-nine. Money doesn't grow on trees, you know.

ACADEMIC: I'm sorry. How about a drink? I've got some whiskey.

PR GIRL: Have you got anything to eat? That's what I really want.

ACADEMIC: Don't know. I don't know if I can help you there. [*He goes away in search of something.*] What with teaching our summer school on communal conflict and marking exams—you wouldn't believe how time-consuming marking is—and no fucking student seems to be able to string a fucking sentence together nowadays—and preparing for next year—I haven't got to the shops—hang on, eureka! [*He comes back with a packet of crisps.*] How about ... ? [*He reads from the packet.*] A packet of Kenny's Triple K, Tangy Salt 'n' Vinegar.

PR GIRL: I don't like those ones.

ACADEMIC: I might have pickled onion as well.

PR GIRL: Triple K?

ACADEMIC: Probably.

PR GIRL: Don't like them either.

ACADEMIC: I thought you were hungry?

PR GIRL: Not for Kenny's Triple K.

ACADEMIC: But don't they do exactly what it says on the packet? 'Kenny's Triple K—Keeps the Hungry Wolf at Bay.'

PR GIRL: Nah—'Kenny's Triple K—Takes Your Tongue Away.' They're like baked Vim.

ACADEMIC: Are they?

PR GIRL: Skin the inside of your mouth, so they do.

ACADEMIC: Oh—goodbye Triple K, so farewell then.

[*He bowls the crisps overarm into the darkness.*]

PR GIRL: You're a loon but a lovely one.

ACADEMIC: You've got absolutely gorgeous knees.

PR GIRL: My mother never let me play rough games in the street. Didn't want them scarred.

ACADEMIC: There's a film about a man who worships a woman's knees.

PR GIRL: I bet that's really interesting.

[*He bends and kisses her knees.*]

ACADEMIC: I could worship yours.

PR GIRL: That would mean ignoring the rest of me.

ACADEMIC: You want to be worshipped.

PR GIRL: Aye, among other things.

[*He kneels up to her. He kisses her mouth.*]

***

She lies under a cover on the sofa. He is in the darkness with a candle looking for something.

ACADEMIC: This will teach me to throw good food around. Ah,

here it is. [*He returns with the crisps he bowled away earlier.*] I always
have to eat ... after.

PR GIRL: You can't eat those.

ACADEMIC: Can't I?

PR GIRL: No.

ACADEMIC: But I'm famished.

PR GIRL: Don't eat them.

ACADEMIC: What if they were the last in the world?

PR GIRL: I'd still say you couldn't.

ACADEMIC: And are you still hungry?

PR GIRL: Famished.

ACADEMIC: We could go and get something, I suppose.

PR GIRL: I'll have to ring home and check on Luke first, but that'd
be great.

[*He lifts cover and peers at her naked body using the candle to see.*]

ACADEMIC: Do you know you're gorgeous?

PR GIRL: Do you mind not dripping wax on me? [*He drops the cover.
She starts to get dressed underneath.*] How many bedrooms did
you say you've got?

ACADEMIC: Three.

PR GIRL: Three.

ACADEMIC: And a boxroom. This is a big old-fashioned flat. There's
another sitting room that I hardly use and there's the garden
as well. It's a house really, just on the level.

PR GIRL: Luke would like it here.

ACADEMIC: Would he? But he's three.

PR GIRL: He likes old places and fine things.

ACADEMIC: You'll have to bring him over.

PR GIRL: Do you have television?

ACADEMIC: Yeah, a portable, why?

PR GIRL: Does it work?

ACADEMIC: Of course. I watch football on it.

PR GIRL: He could even ... spend the night. Have you got a
hairbrush? [*He goes into the darkness. She gets out from under the
cover. He trips and falls.*] Are you all right?

ACADEMIC: It's nothing. I've just knocked a pile of records over.

PR GIRL: Records. In case you haven't heard, it's CDs now.

ACADEMIC: I can never throw anything away. It's a bit of a problem.

PR GIRL: Can't you put the records in a box? On a shelf?

[*He comes back.*]

ACADEMIC: Here. [*He hands her the hairbrush. It has soft bristles.*] Want to tidy me and my place up, do you? [*She brushes her hair.*]

PR GIRL: No. Yes.

ACADEMIC: Well, why don't you bring him then? We could try an evening together, the three of us.

PR GIRL: He'd love that. It'd be like a wee holiday for him. When suits?

ACADEMIC: What suits you?

PR GIRL: This weekend coming?

ACADEMIC: No, I'm busy.

PR GIRL: Well, whenever. [*She hands the hairbrush back to him.*] Right, I'm ready.

ACADEMIC: But—the weekend after, you're on.

PR GIRL: Give me that. [*She takes back the brush and uses it on the shoulders and lapels of his jacket.*] You need sprucing up. Me and Luke, we're taking you shopping when we come. There, that'll do for now.

ACADEMIC: Right, let's go.

PR GIRL: Oh, my tights.

ACADEMIC: Well remembered.

PR GIRL: Can you fetch them, please?

[*He retrieves them from behind the sofa. They go in her handbag.*]

PR GIRL: Hope my mother doesn't spot my bare legs. She always says, if the tights are off, it only means one thing.

ACADEMIC: I thought you were ringing her?

PR GIRL: I was. But then our house is tiny and I thought I'd wake Luke. So I thought, leave it. He's safe. Let's just go out and have a nice time.

ACADEMIC: Hang on, got to do the candles.

[*They go around the room blowing candles out.*]

PR GIRL: The last is mine. [*He holds the last candle up to her. She blows it out.*] Did you make a wish?

ACADEMIC: No.

PR GIRL: I did.

[*They leave.*]

8 THE ACADEMIC AND THE SPOKESWOMAN

A bedroom in a hotel by the sea. Sound of waves on a nearby beach. ACADEMIC *comes in with a couple of suitcases, a holdall and a shoulder bag. He drops everything and flicks the light switch. The bulb blows.* SPOKESWOMAN *follows.*

ACADEMIC: Bloody hell.

SPOKESWOMAN: What is it?

ACADEMIC: Light bulb's gone.

SPOKESWOMAN: In the old Soviet Union the well-prepared traveller always had a light bulb. Have you?

ACADEMIC: No, I haven't.

SPOKESWOMAN: Why not?

ACADEMIC: Possibly because light bulbs aren't in short supply in occupied Ireland.

SPOKESWOMAN: So unfunny. [*She notices something outside.*] Will you look at that? [SPOKESWOMAN *goes down on her knees.*]

ACADEMIC: What are you doing?

SPOKESWOMAN: I'm on my knees.

ACADEMIC: I see that but I'm over here, Lewinsky.

SPOKESWOMAN: Will you look at that sea?

ACADEMIC: Yes.

SPOKESWOMAN: When you see something like that, you have to go down in front of it.

ACADEMIC: Can a man produce this effect?

SPOKESWOMAN: Look at it, Robert, doesn't that touch you?

ACADEMIC: It's very nice.

SPOKESWOMAN: Come and join me.

ACADEMIC: Do I have to?

SPOKESWOMAN: Yes, you do. Come here.

ACADEMIC: I doubt this'll work. I mislaid my faith on a train home from Derry in '72.

SPOKESWOMAN: This is nothing to do with faith. [*He kneels beside her and slips an arm around her.*] Do you ever think of anything else?

ACADEMIC: My work. Politics.

SPOKESWOMAN: Well think about something else for a change. Look at the ocean.

ACADEMIC: I thought you'd given all this up?

SPOKESWOMAN: All what?

ACADEMIC: Being religious.

SPOKESWOMAN: You are impossible. [*She stands up.*] I only gave up the Catholic church. My awe remains intact.

ACADEMIC: Oh, right. [*He stands.*] I suppose once the church has you in its teeth, that's it. You go on kneeling and praying, but just pretend it's nature not God.

SPOKESWOMAN: You haven't a clue, have you? Can you put that bag on the bed?

ACADEMIC: Why don't you educate me?

   [*He lifts suitcase onto bed.*]

SPOKESWOMAN: I've long since realised that's a hopeless task.

   [*She unzips the suitcase and begins to search for something in it.*]

ACADEMIC: But I thought you liked me.

SPOKESWOMAN: Of course I like you. And part of liking is accepting the other for what they are.

ACADEMIC: You have to like someone to sleep with them?

SPOKESWOMAN: Of course you do. We're not about to have a crisis, are we, about us?

ACADEMIC: I hope not.

SPOKESWOMAN: Me too. Would you put the other on the bed please?

ACADEMIC: By the way, nice television gig last week.

   [*He lifts the second suitcase onto bed.*]

SPOKESWOMAN: It was a nightmare.

   [*She unzips it and begins searching.*]

ACADEMIC: But why wasn't the woman shouting 'liar' at you thrown out?

SPOKESWOMAN: Please, let's not discuss it. It was a nightmare.

ACADEMIC: All right, you choose what you want to talk about.

SPOKESWOMAN: Well, you must be delighted you've got me here.

ACADEMIC: I seem to remember this was your idea.

SPOKESWOMAN: Oh yes, I forgot and what a marvellous choice I made. One could be inspired in a place like this. If one had the talent one could write—poetry—as I have seen some do.

ACADEMIC: You've been here before?

SPOKESWOMAN: Correct.

ACADEMIC: When?

SPOKESWOMAN: Long before you. Now where's it gone?

ACADEMIC: Not with Cathal?

SPOKESWOMAN: Yeah.

ACADEMIC: Oh no.

[*She rummages in the first suitcase again.*]

SPOKESWOMAN: You know I worshipped him.

ACADEMIC: So you tell me.

SPOKESWOMAN: Do I bore you? Sorry. Shall I go?

ACADEMIC: You don't bore me. It's just ... can we leave him out of it?

SPOKESWOMAN: Of course, and it is true he was mad—the relationship would never have lasted.

ACADEMIC: You think so?

SPOKESWOMAN: Come here. [*He goes over.*] Kiss me. [*They embrace. She kisses him passionately.*] Okay, goodnight.

ACADEMIC: Sorry.

SPOKESWOMAN: I'm going to bed when I find what I'm looking for.

ACADEMIC: Isn't that bed for both of us?

SPOKESWOMAN: Not tonight. Go down to the desk. I'm sure they can fix you up with something. You don't want to be with me anyway. [*She searches the second suitcase again.*]

ACADEMIC: Can I give you a tip? [*He turns on the bedside light.*] Light's always useful when looking for something.

SPOKESWOMAN: Ah, clever you, and here it is.

[*She takes out a battered brass box.*]

ACADEMIC: Oh no.

SPOKESWOMAN: Yes, Cathal's stash box. Sorry, it had to come.

ACADEMIC: Why on earth have you brought that?

SPOKESWOMAN: It's a *memento mori.*

ACADEMIC: 'Remember you must die.' You need to be reminded?

SPOKESWOMAN: Is that what that means?

ACADEMIC: Yeah.

SPOKESWOMAN: I thought it was a reminder of someone dead?

ACADEMIC: No. That would be 'Quis momens mori Cathali' – 'This reminds me of Cathal.'

SPOKESWOMAN: Oh ... well, my Latin was always poor ... anyway, he was killed, and this reminds me of my mortality.

ACADEMIC: Oh no, here we go.

SPOKESWOMAN: Meaning what?

ACADEMIC:There was that little melodramatic throb in your voice. You're going to die in your bed, darling, of natural causes.

SPOKESWOMAN: Oh.

ACADEMIC: Not like him. Of gunshot wounds courtesy of some loyalist.

SPOKESWOMAN: Run by British Intelligence, don't forget ...

ACADEMIC: Yeah, yeah, whatever.

SPOKESWOMAN: You can't be completely sure.

ACADEMIC: You're with the angels. You've abandoned war. Or do you know something I don't know yet?

SPOKESWOMAN: No, still on track, or we were last time I looked.

[ACADEMIC *takes the stash box.*]

ACADEMIC: Why do you keep this? He's been dead for twelve years.

SPOKESWOMAN: Obviously, there's an unresolved grief issue here. You see that's what thirty years of war does. It fucks you up.

[*She takes back the stash box and puts it on the bureau by the bed.*]

ACADEMIC: Can I be blunt?

SPOKESWOMAN: Have you ever not been?

ACADEMIC: Why don't you get your head shrunk?

SPOKESWOMAN: What?

ACADEMIC: Allow someone to delve inside your skull, snip a few wires and nail you shut again? It'd do you the world of good.

SPOKESWOMAN: That's beyond the pale. Now you really can't stay.

ACADEMIC: Why not?

SPOKESWOMAN: You're saying I'm mad.

ACADEMIC: No, I'm not.

SPOKESWOMAN: Not in so many words but you are. Go on, away to the desk with you. Get your own room.

ACADEMIC: I didn't come away to sleep apart. I came to be with you and ... to talk to you.

SPOKESWOMAN: What about?

ACADEMIC: Nothing, in particular, I just, you know, want ... conversation.

SPOKESWOMAN: Then we need a lighter first. Have you got yours?

[*He feels in his pockets.*]

ACADEMIC: Don't know ... thought I had ...

SPOKESWOMAN: You always have your lighter.

ACADEMIC: I know.

[*He upends his shoulder bag tumbling books and papers onto the table.*]

SPOKESWOMAN: Make yourself at home, don't you worry about any mess.

ACADEMIC: Yes. [*He finds his lighter and throws it to her.*]

SPOKESWOMAN: Lock the door would you? We don't want to be disturbed. [*She gets into bed on the same side as the stash box. He locks the door.*] Come here. Come and sit down. [*He sits. She takes a joint from the stash box.*] Not so far away. [*He stretches out beside her but on top of the covers.*] Now, what exactly do you want to talk about?

ACADEMIC: Nothing.

SPOKESWOMAN: Oh, I think you do.

ACADEMIC: Where would you get an idea like that?

SPOKESWOMAN: Well, you did say you wanted to talk.

ACADEMIC: In general, but not about anything in particular. [*She lights the joint she holds. The joint goes backwards and forwards during the exchange that follows.*] Do you ever imagine what the brothers would say if you were caught?

SPOKESWOMAN: What brothers?

ACADEMIC: *The* brothers.

SPOKESWOMAN: Please, I haven't come all this way to be reminded.

ACADEMIC: But don't you ever worry about them?

SPOKESWOMAN: No.

ACADEMIC: Do you ever think someone might tout?

SPOKESWOMAN: No.

ACADEMIC: Never?

SPOKESWOMAN: Do you not think I'm not extraordinarily careful?

ACADEMIC: But if you were caught what would you do?

SPOKESWOMAN: I'd brazen it out.

ACADEMIC: But your organisation is connected to an organisation that kneecaps dealers.

SPOKESWOMAN: But not for drugs—for their woeful driving and bad haircuts.

ACADEMIC: Really.

SPOKESWOMAN: There's no double standards involved in this, promise.

ACADEMIC: If you say so.

SPOKESWOMAN: I am the public face of an organisation that is making the difficult transition from armed struggle to ordinary, grubby politics. I am under a great deal of pressure. This is how I relax. And if anyone doesn't like what I do, and it doesn't matter who they are, they can go to hell.

ACADEMIC: I'm with you there, pet.

SPOKESWOMAN: Shush, listen.

ACADEMIC: What?

SPOKESWOMAN: Can you hear it?

ACADEMIC: No, what? Oh yeah. I can hear it. Your breathing.

SPOKESWOMAN: No, the sea.

ACADEMIC: That's not the sea.

SPOKESWOMAN: Listen. It is.

ACADEMIC: That's the lift.

SPOKESWOMAN: No, it isn't. Those are breaking waves.

ACADEMIC: Only in your head.

SPOKESWOMAN: What are you saying?

ACADEMIC: Man, you can't hold your pot.

SPOKESWOMAN: Pot! Who ever came up with pot?

ACADEMIC: I dunno. I know a man I could ask, though. A lexi ... a lexi ...

SPOKESWOMAN: Go on boy, you can do it.

ACADEMIC:. A lexi ... cog ... rap.

SPOKESWOMAN: Her. [*They roar with laughter.*] Are you sure you don't want to tell me you're sleeping with someone?

ACADEMIC: No.

SPOKESWOMAN: No you're not or no you don't want to tell?

ACADEMIC: Neither. God I hate these interrogations.

SPOKESWOMAN: I think you've found someone.

ACADEMIC: That's rubbish.

SPOKESWOMAN: I have a nose for these things. You have, haven't you?

ACADEMIC: Of course not.

SPOKESWOMAN: You have. Look at the way your Adam's Apple's bobbing. That's a sure sign, Robert, of infidelity. That, and your general manner which is shifty and has been for weeks.

ACADEMIC: I don't know what you're talking about.

SPOKESWOMAN: Oh well, not to worry. I've found someone else too.

ACADEMIC: I don't believe you.

SPOKESWOMAN: You're right.

ACADEMIC: You wouldn't have come if that were true.

SPOKESWOMAN: That's right. I'm straight and I'm committed and I'm loyal and I don't want to be fucked around. I'm too old, too tired and I can't be arsed with it.

ACADEMIC: Of course.

SPOKESWOMAN: But I am being arsed about here.

ACADEMIC: No, you're not.

SPOKESWOMAN: But the little woman inside says I am.

ACADEMIC: She's wrong.

SPOKESWOMAN: She's never wrong.

ACADEMIC: She is.

SPOKESWOMAN: I don't believe you. Now, I can understand why you won't talk. You know I don't want to be dumped. But if I am, so be it. I can take it. I won't hate you. However, you have only twenty-four hours to come clean. If you're lying and we get back to the city and I catch the pair of you, my anger will be biblical. So let's have an adult conversation now. I'll be civilised. I won't make you go to another room. I was just codding before. Just get it out.

ACADEMIC: All right.

SPOKESWOMAN: I was right. Who is she?

ACADEMIC: Now, you're wrong there.

SPOKESWOMAN: I don't think so. Who is she?

ACADEMIC: He.

SPOKESWOMAN: He! Oh no, even I've got limits.

ACADEMIC: He. And now I'll have to break our agreement.

SPOKESWOMAN: Which one?

ACADEMIC: To stay off politics.

SPOKESWOMAN: What we agreed was we wouldn't argue or score points.

ACADEMIC: I'm not scoring points now.

SPOKESWOMAN: Go on.

ACADEMIC: Ten Rounds Milligan.

SPOKESWOMAN: I don't believe it. This is what you want to talk about?

ACADEMIC: I heard something about him.

SPOKESWOMAN: He's old news. He's out of the loop.

ACADEMIC: He isn't anymore. He's making bombs. You didn't know? No, I don't suppose they'd tell you. That makes sense.

SPOKESWOMAN: Unusually, you're actually being tedious.

ACADEMIC: And some of your people are happy to let him go ahead. They really haven't told you this?

SPOKESWOMAN: No, they haven't. They've nothing to tell.

ACADEMIC: It's for dissidents.

SPOKESWOMAN: Fuck off.

ACADEMIC: They'll take responsibility.

SPOKESWOMAN: Fuck off.

ACADEMIC: But your people'll be happy.

SPOKESWOMAN: Fuck off.

ACADEMIC: Happy days, still hitting the Brits, they'll say.

SPOKESWOMAN: Fuck off.

ACADEMIC: Privately, *sotto voce*, of course.

SPOKESWOMAN: Fuck off.

ACADEMIC: And the beauty is ... everyone's so terrified of everything unravelling ...

SPOKESWOMAN: Fuck off.

ACADEMIC: He won't be touched.

SPOKESWOMAN: Fuck off.

ACADEMIC: He can't be arrested and tried. It would destroy everything.

SPOKESWOMAN: Fuck off.

ACADEMIC: So nothing will happen.

SPOKESWOMAN: Fuck off.

ACADEMIC: And the rest as they say will be history.

SPOKESWOMAN: Have you finished?

ACADEMIC: Yes.

SPOKESWOMAN: Are you as naive as you seem? Or are you just pretending? Or is it you just don't get out enough and have lost contact with reality?

ACADEMIC: Oh the wit's as razor sharp as ever, I see.

SPOKESWOMAN: Do you really expect me to know every rumour about every grimy little hood that walks the streets.

ACADEMIC: This is a bit more than than.

SPOKESWOMAN: I'd go fucking crazy if I took up every story that came my way.

ACADEMIC: No you wouldn't.

SPOKESWOMAN: What?

ACADEMIC: Of course you wouldn't. You're mad already.

SPOKESWOMAN: You know we're all just trying to make something work. We don't know everything, we don't always succeed either. We are all just swimmers in the same murky sea. Is that clear enough for you?

ACADEMIC: I think so.

SPOKESWOMAN: Once more for clarity.

ACADEMIC: Oh why not.

SPOKESWOMAN: For God's sake, you and this story—fuck off.

ACADEMIC: Oh good—that's sorted that then. [*They laugh.*]

SPOKESWOMAN: Imagine if it could always be like that. It'd be so brilliant. When are you de-commissioning?

ACADEMIC: Fuck off.

SPOKESWOMAN: Is the war over?

ACADEMIC: Fuck off.

SPOKESWOMAN: Is your party president a member of the Army Council?

ACADEMIC: Fuck off.

SPOKESWOMAN: So it isn't true you've found someone, Robert?

ACADEMIC: Fuck off.

SPOKESWOMAN: Get up.

ACADEMIC: Why?

SPOKESWOMAN: Just do what I say for once? [*He stands. She puts the joint in the ashtray and throws back the covers.*] Get in.

ACADEMIC: There's never a dull moment with you.

[*He gets in beside her. She pulls the covers over them.*]

SPOKESWOMAN: I know, I am quite wonderful.

ACADEMIC: Modest too.

SPOKESWOMAN: Oh yes, that as well. [*She embraces* ACADEMIC.] Come on.

ACADEMIC: You've still got your clothes on.

SPOKESWOMAN: I can't be bothered to take them off.

ACADEMIC: I love it when you strip.

SPOKESWOMAN: I'll do it for you later.

***

SPOKESWOMAN: Your mind really wasn't on that?

ACADEMIC: Oh, fuck off will you.

9 THE SPOKESWOMAN AND THE OFFICIAL

SPOKESWOMAN *sits up on the bed. She leans against a bank of pillows. There is an armchair.* OFFICIAL *calls 'Hello' through the door.*

SPOKESWOMAN: Come in.

[OFFICIAL *enters. He wears a suit. He carries a laptop case.*]

OFFICIAL: Sorry to barge in.

SPOKESWOMAN: Don't be sorry. I'm the one who made you come here.

OFFICIAL: But then I did ask to see you. I need to talk.

SPOKESWOMAN: Yes, generally we do.

OFFICIAL: About Ten Rounds ... Mr. Milligan ... I'm afraid.

SPOKESWOMAN: Oh no, don't ruin everything. I don't want to hear about him. He's a terrible fellow. Let's just chat for a bit.

OFFICIAL: All right. Who was that then who let me in?

SPOKESWOMAN: My mother.

OFFICIAL: You share the house?

SPOKESWOMAN: No! She's just round because I'm ill. She'll be off soon.

OFFICIAL: There's a resemblance you know.

SPOKESWOMAN: Not too much I hope.

OFFICIAL: Oh no. You'd just know you're both from the same gene pool.

SPOKESWOMAN: Don't lurk over there. Close the door. Come right in.

OFFICIAL: You won't bite?

SPOKESWOMAN: I nip sometimes—nicely—but I don't bite.

[*He steps forward.*]

OFFICIAL: That's good to know.

SPOKESWOMAN: Did someone say I did?

OFFICIAL: No.

SPOKESWOMAN: Good, I don't like to hear ill spoken of me.

OFFICIAL: Speaking of which, you're ill yourself?

SPOKESWOMAN: Oh, nothing serious really. Just dying. Sit down.

OFFICIAL: Aren't we all?

[*He sits on an armchair balancing the laptop on his knees.*]

SPOKESWOMAN: That's why we have to seize life with both hands.

OFFICIAL: Live hard and wild?

SPOKESWOMAN: And I am wild.

OFFICIAL: So what exactly is the matter?

SPOKESWOMAN: Didn't I say I'm dying? Other than that it's a sore throat.

OFFICIAL: Slight. I hope.

SPOKESWOMAN: The old larynx is just exhausted. It's all the yacking I have to do.

OFFICIAL: You don't smoke?

SPOKESWOMAN: Of course I don't. It's unhealthy.

OFFICIAL: I watched the programme last week. Impressive.

SPOKESWOMAN: Tell me more. I love to hear about me.

OFFICIAL: Those programmes where the people meet the movers and shakers are tricky. The public have to be controlled and the floppy haired compère couldn't do it.

SPOKESWOMAN: There are worse than him.

OFFICIAL: He didn't do very well with the woman heckler.

SPOKESWOMAN: No.

OFFICIAL: Was she shouting 'liar' at you?

SPOKESWOMAN: Aye.

OFFICIAL: Floppy should have stopped her.

SPOKESWOMAN: But he didn't. Madwomen make good telly, you see.

OFFICIAL: She didn't. She was awful.

SPOKESWOMAN: I tried to speak to her afterwards in the hospitality suite.

OFFICIAL: And?

SPOKESWOMAN: She just put her drink down and walked out.

OFFICIAL: She should try listening.

SPOKESWOMAN: If you're bitter, it's hard to break with the habit of centuries.

OFFICIAL: But you have to. I'd say, in my work, listening is eighty percent of the job.

SPOKESWOMAN: We're a good fit then.

OFFICIAL: How's that?

SPOKESWOMAN: I'm the talker. You're the listener.

OFFICIAL: Oh, I see.

SPOKESWOMAN: You're not nervous are you?

OFFICIAL: No.

SPOKESWOMAN: You seem nervous.

OFFICIAL: No, I'm not.

SPOKESWOMAN: Were you nervous the first time we met?

OFFICIAL: Those talks were a big deal. Of course I was. Weren't you?

SPOKESWOMAN: No.

OFFICIAL: Oh, cool eh?

SPOKESWOMAN: Maybe a bit. But what I remember most was how impressive and ... fair you were.

OFFICIAL: Thank you.

SPOKESWOMAN: That doesn't alarm you, does it?

OFFICIAL: Not at all.

SPOKESWOMAN: I also noticed that you would keep looking at me, at the first meeting and at all the ones that followed.

OFFICIAL: Yes.

SPOKESWOMAN: You were?

OFFICIAL: Yes.

SPOKESWOMAN: You know meetings, you're bored, idle thoughts cross your mind?

OFFICIAL: Yes.

SPOKESWOMAN: I wonder if our thoughts were wandering in the same direction?

OFFICIAL: I don't know.

SPOKESWOMAN: I think they were.

OFFICIAL: If you say so.

SPOKESWOMAN: I do. And that's nothing to be ashamed about. It's normal. Healthy.

OFFICIAL: Under our narrow crust we are wild animals. We are the sum of our desires.

SPOKESWOMAN: Are you a philosopher?

OFFICIAL: Not really.

SPOKESWOMAN: But you like to think, don't you? You're a thinker, I think.

OFFICIAL: I wouldn't go so far as to say.

SPOKESWOMAN: Don't belittle yourself. When you sit in a room with someone for as long as I sat with you, you get to know them rather well. Just by watching. You're a thinker.

OFFICIAL: Thank you.

SPOKESWOMAN: You can't imagine how delighted I was when I was told we had to meet regularly and ah ... keep the channels of communication open. I've found our exchanges really useful. I've found you open, intelligent and adroit.

OFFICIAL: Thank you again.

[*A door bangs off stage.*]

SPOKESWOMAN: There goes my mother. Do you mind sitting on the bed? There'll be less strain on my voice that way. [*He moves to the bed. The laptop comes with him.*] Do you have a girlfriend? No. Sorry. I take that back.

OFFICIAL: I don't mind answering. No.

SPOKESWOMAN: Really. No one?

OFFICIAL: I have some friends but not really, as such, a girlfriend, I'm ...

SPOKESWOMAN: Someone who doesn't like to be tied? Who likes to have casual relationships?

OFFICIAL: Who's not really in a proper relationship, I was going to say.

SPOKESWOMAN: At the moment?

OFFICIAL: Correct.

SPOKESWOMAN: How old are you? Actually, sorry, I don't want to know.

OFFICIAL: Why?

SPOKESWOMAN: You might ask me my age then.

OFFICIAL: Oh, and what's wrong with that?

SPOKESWOMAN: Well I'm not telling you.

OFFICIAL: Does it matter?

SPOKESWOMAN: Yes.

OFFICIAL: I thought age didn't matter anymore.

SPOKESWOMAN: You thought wrong. It does matter because it's horrible.

OFFICIAL: Is it?

SPOKESWOMAN: It's one of the great Hollywood lies that age brings lustre to a woman, to anyone. Jerry Hall—fifty and frisky, Joan Collins—sixty and sexy. Shite. Age brings only decrepitude and death. There's nothing good to be said for it. You're looking at me in a funny way.

OFFICIAL: Am I?

SPOKESWOMAN: Yes. Is something the matter? Don't you agree?

OFFICIAL: No, it's just one doesn't imagine having this sort of conversation.

SPOKESWOMAN: With someone like me ... with my politics.

OFFICIAL: Yes.

SPOKESWOMAN: But I'm more than just my politics. That's what I hate about my role. Everyone thinks I'm just a republican. Nothing else. Absolute bollocks.

OFFICIAL: The titles is one thing, the book quite another.

SPOKESWOMAN: Yes. How well you put it.

[*She gets out of bed.*]

OFFICIAL: Thank you.

[*She walks to the door and locks it.*]

SPOKESWOMAN: And yet you think of yourself as mostly a listener rather than a speaker?

OFFICIAL: I do.

SPOKESWOMAN: There's no one here but I've locked the door anyhow. We don't want to be disturbed.

OFFICIAL: No.

SPOKESWOMAN: Now, what do we need to talk about today?

OFFICIAL: Ten Rounds ... Mr. Milligan.

SPOKESWOMAN: Oh yes, so we do. I'd forgotten [*She takes the laptop from his lap.*] Why don't you let me have this? You can't be comfortable holding it. [*She puts the laptop on the armchair.*] Is there anything important on this?

OFFICIAL: Only everything.

SPOKESWOMAN: Well, nothing's going to happen to it there on the chair.

OFFICIAL: I have a great dread of losing my laptop.

SPOKESWOMAN: I suppose you would.

OFFICIAL: You know over the years you read of these idiots, policemen and soldiers and civil servants, who leave their laptops in their cars and then the cars are stolen and then all the information on the laptop ...

SPOKESWOMAN: I know—would have come to us.

OFFICIAL: That's a great fear.

SPOKESWOMAN: It's not going to happen today. And if it did we wouldn't look. We'd give it straight back. It and you are safe.

OFFICIAL: Oh good.

SPOKESWOMAN: So what precisely is the problem?

OFFICIAL: Oh, our friend, yes.

SPOKESWOMAN: He's no friend of mine.

OFFICIAL: He's a bollocks, frankly.

SPOKESWOMAN: Tell me in your own words, not mine.

OFFICIAL: He's chucking paint over drug dealers' houses and burning their cars. He's dragging hoods to what he calls his 'Stew Room' and beating them. Whenever there's trouble on the streets, he organises the petrol bombs and barricades. Someone will be killed, eventually. So before that happens we want to take him out of circulation.

SPOKESWOMAN: You mean, revoke his license, put him back in jail?

OFFICIAL: Yes.

SPOKESWOMAN: Because of what he's done, or might do?

OFFICIAL: Bit of both.

SPOKESWOMAN: Either what he's done justifies pulling him up or it doesn't. You can't take him because of what he might do. It looks bad.

OFFICIAL: Well, we have a duty to act now to prevent worse.

SPOKESWOMAN: No, your first duty is to think. You arrest him—his friends will be on the streets in half an hour.

OFFICIAL: A little trouble now is better than a lot later on.

SPOKESWOMAN: Sorry, wrong. This way lies disaster. The agreement promised this sort of thing wouldn't happen. You lock him up and everyone's going to go, 'Oh, they're still locking republicans away when they feel like it.'

OFFICIAL: Not because we feel like it, because he's …

SPOKESWOMAN: What?

OFFICIAL: Out of control. Inciting disorder.

SPOKESWOMAN: What—and there aren't loyalists doing the same?

OFFICIAL: So what.

SPOKESWOMAN: Think. They're queuing up round our way to kick the shite out of the agreement. You scoop up Milligan and you give 'em another reason. If he'd been handling explosives or something like that and you pulled him in, it mightn't be liked but it would be understood. But he isn't. So you act and it's going to look like pure badness. Come on. It's hard enough for us selling this as it is. Why make it harder?

OFFICIAL: Because in our judgement, we must have him.

SPOKESWOMAN: In which case—you'll risk riots and who knows what?—because of some idiot acting hard on the streets. You sat through the first meeting between us and you, and the ones that followed. Look how far we've travelled? You saw that TV programme. The woman who heckled hated me but nobody died. That has to be better than before. [*She sits on the bed.*] If we break the necklace now we'll never get the pearls back on the string.

OFFICIAL: I can't go back and say that.

SPOKESWOMAN: Of course not. Let us handle this. He'll be ordered to leave. I give you my word.

OFFICIAL: He's to be out by Friday.

SPOKESWOMAN: Friday it is.

OFFICIAL: Which is in forty-eight hours.

SPOKESWOMAN: I understand when Friday is. Now, I said he'll be gone and I gave my word. Now I have to know you won't do anything beforehand. [*He shakes his head.*] Say it.

OFFICIAL: Nothing happens until after Friday.

SPOKESWOMAN: You can kiss me now.

OFFICIAL: I can?

SPOKESWOMAN: Yes.

OFFICIAL: I have to, do I?

SPOKESWOMAN: Yes, you do. You must. [*He kisses her.*] I wish I'd never laid eyes on you.

OFFICIAL: Do you? Why?

SPOKESWOMAN: You're going to make me unhappy.

OFFICIAL: No, I'm not.

SPOKESWOMAN: Aren't you? Do you promise?

OFFICIAL: Yes.

SPOKESWOMAN: Do you know, you denied it but I think you are a bit nervous of me?

OFFICIAL: No, I'm not. If anyone's nervous it's you.

SPOKESWOMAN: Why?

OFFICIAL: You're the one coming on.

SPOKESWOMAN: Why don't we even things up. Why don't you ask me for something? Anything you want. Anything.

OFFICIAL: I think I'd like to go.

SPOKESWOMAN: Why?

OFFICIAL: And come back tonight.

SPOKESWOMAN: Why?

OFFICIAL: It's nicer at night.

SPOKESWOMAN: Is it?

OFFICIAL: Yes. I think so.

SPOKESWOMAN: There's no one here. And even if there was they couldn't get in.

OFFICIAL: I don't really like it in the morning.

SPOKESWOMAN: Oh.

OFFICIAL: I like a meal, a drink or two, and then events can take their natural course.

SPOKESWOMAN: Oh, very conventional.

OFFICIAL: I can't help it. It's the way I am.

SPOKESWOMAN: Nor can I help the way I am. I'm sorry. I can't wait. [*She moves onto his lap.*] Your leg's shaking.

OFFICIAL: Is it?

SPOKESWOMAN: Yes.

OFFICIAL: Well, it would. Under these circumstances.

SPOKESWOMAN: We'll have to stop that. [*She puts her arms around him.*] If it's too light just close your eyes. [*She closes his lids with her fingertips.*] There, you see, night, total blackout.
[*They begin to stroke each other.*]

OFFICIAL: You will do it?

SPOKESWOMAN: What?

OFFICIAL: Sort our problem?

SPOKESWOMAN: I said, I will …
[*She stops his mouth with hers.*]

***

SPOKESWOMAN *pulls on a nightdress and then dressing gown and* OFFICIAL *buttons himself up.*

OFFICIAL: Feeling better now?

SPOKESWOMAN: I'm not certain that's a nice question.

OFFICIAL: I meant your throat.

SPOKESWOMAN: Oh. I thought you meant it in another sense.
[*The door bangs again far away.*]

OFFICIAL: Am I right to trust you? You've only got 'til Friday, you know.

SPOKESWOMAN: After what we've just done you really think I'm going to renege?

OFFICIAL: No.

SPOKESWOMAN: Right. Good. [*He picks up his laptop.*] Going?

OFFICIAL: I've think stayed long enough for a formal visit.

SPOKESWOMAN: The next time won't be formal, I promise you. [*She kisses him passionately, then unlocks the door and pushes him out.*] Go on, down the stairs with you. I think I heard my mother come back. [*She follows him out the door.*] I don't want any smirking in front of her. And remember, I'm right behind you.

10 THE OFFICIAL AND THE PROSTITUTE

Morning. PROSTITUTE *lies on or in her bed, asleep, breathing evenly. Her clothes lie on the floor.* OFFICIAL, *fully dressed, sleeps in the armchair. Sunlight shines through the window and falls on him. He is sweating. There are bottles lying about. The television is on. We hear a medley of sounds from the set—a band parade, a roaring crowd, a line of policemen beating their truncheons on their shields, a wailing ambulance siren. The soundtrack of civil disorder.* OFFICIAL *stirs and rubs his eyes. He wakes.*

OFFICIAL: Oh my head. [*He looks at* PROSTITUTE.] Hello, hello over there.

[PROSTITUTE *wakes.*]

PROSTITUTE: You're still here.

OFFICIAL: Have you got the remote?

PROSTITUTE: Somewhere.

OFFICIAL: Will you turn that thing off?

[*She searches for the remote in her bed.*]

PROSTITUTE: My daddy always said the box was the death of conversation. He was right. 'Since that thing came along people definitely don't talk the way they used to talk. Now they just chatter.' [*She finds the remote.*] As for the local news, what's the point watching it, I say. It's always the same.

OFFICIAL: Turn it off, now, please.

[*She points the remote. The sound dies.*]

PROSTITUTE: It's funny, many a time I've been in a car with a client and it comes on the news about a bombing or a shooting. They always say they can't do it, not after hearing what's happened. But in the end they always do.

OFFICIAL: And the picture too. I can't bear to have it on. [*She points the remote again.*] Thank you.

PROSTITUTE: Well, good morning. [*He says nothing.*] Is it a good one?

OFFICIAL: I don't know. I would doubt it. No, it isn't.

PROSTITUTE: Are you feeling better?

OFFICIAL: I have no idea. Worse, probably.

PROSTITUTE: What was the matter, do you know?

OFFICIAL: The matter?

PROSTITUTE: Last night. [*He shakes his head.*] Funny thing the body. One minute, nothing, the next right as rain.

OFFICIAL: This is women's wisdom, is it?

PROSTITUTE: Throw us me fags, would you?

[*He throws her the packet and the lighter. She lights up.*]

OFFICIAL: Do you know what stress is?

PROSTITUTE: Yeah, this job. Pure stress. Why'd you think I need a fag first thing?

OFFICIAL: I'm under a lot of stress.

PROSTITUTE: Have a cigarette.

OFFICIAL: I don't want one.

PROSTITUTE: Come on, try one. It'll do you good.

OFFICIAL: I don't want a cigarette.

PROSTITUTE: But smoking is good for you. Obviously it's bad as well but it does calm you down.

OFFICIAL: I said I don't want one.

PROSTITUTE: Do you know what I think?

OFFICIAL: What?

PROSTITUTE: I think we should try again.

OFFICIAL: No.

PROSTITUTE: You'd a lot to drink.

OFFICIAL: It wasn't the drink.

PROSTITUTE: Wasn't it?

OFFICIAL: No.

PROSTITUTE: You were well jarred. Well, so was I. I can hardly talk.

OFFICIAL: It wasn't the drink.

PROSTITUTE: What was it then? Are you married?

OFFICIAL: Of course not.

PROSTITUTE: No, I can't imagine you married.

OFFICIAL: Why do you say that?

PROSTITUTE: You don't seem like the marrying kind.

OFFICIAL: Exactly. I'm not.

PROSTITUTE: So what's there to fret about? You're a free bird. You can do what you want. [*He shakes his head.*] So why don't you tell me about it?

OFFICIAL: Tell you what?

PROSTITUTE: I did my dance of the seven veils. Why weren't you excited?

OFFICIAL: Because I'm bloody depressed is why.

PROSTITUTE: Why are you depressed?

OFFICIAL: I just am.

PROSTITUTE: Go on, you can tell me.

OFFICIAL: Just, because.

PROSTITUTE: Are you religious?

OFFICIAL: Good God no.

PROSTITUTE: I was, when I was a little girl. Since when, as you can see, I've taken a different path.

OFFICIAL: I never had any religious feelings.

PROSTITUTE: I'd like mine back. I wonder sometimes if that'll happen. If I'll wake up and that'll be it, I'll be back on the straight and narrow.

OFFICIAL: I don't think it happens like that.

PROSTITUTE: Why not?

OFFICIAL: Because if there is a God He'll have made fucking sure it won't be easy.

PROSTITUTE: A lot of my clients tell me things you know. It does them good.

OFFICIAL: It's good to talk, eh?

PROSTITUTE: Yeah.

OFFICIAL: You weren't paid to listen to my nonsense.

PROSTITUTE: I'm not a Samaritan. This is business. I help you now, you come back later. Go on, talk to me. It won't do you any harm.

[*He points at the television.*]

OFFICIAL: The politicians bicker and squabble endlessly ...

PROSTITUTE: While drawing their salaries and boasting to the whole world how great they are for making peace.

OFFICIAL: Yes, and meantime their people are chucking pipe bombs and burning neighbours out and the politicians don't stop them even though they promised. And we're so frightened of sliding back we all turn a blind eye to it. That's the really horrible part of it.

PROSTITUTE: The mistake was to expect it would be any different.

OFFICIAL: Oh, was it, really?

PROSTITUTE: Look, there are some people make promises they can't keep and never intend to keep. Some people are weasels. It's no good gurning about it.

OFFICIAL: Oh, more women's wisdom.

PROSTITUTE: It's human nature. It can't be changed.

OFFICIAL: What's the alternative? Do nothing and that way avoid disappointment?

PROSTITUTE: No, just don't expect not to be disappointed.

OFFICIAL: Let's talk about something else.

PROSTITUTE: Do you know what your trouble is?

OFFICIAL: Please, let's not go over all that again.

PROSTITUTE: You spend all your time listening. You said so yourself last night. You need to be released.

OFFICIAL: Oh yes, and don't tell me, that can only happen here ...

PROSTITUTE: Yes. Saturdays are good. I'm free, morning and afternoon.

OFFICIAL: I have to go to London some weekends.

PROSTITUTE: I'll come. I'll carry your bag.

OFFICIAL: Now, I've already asked, can we please talk about something else, besides me and my greater happiness? I'm tired of me. I want a holiday from me. Christ, that sun's giving me a headache. [*He goes to the window.*]

PROSTITUTE: All right. You choose. What do you want to talk about? Go on. [*He fiddles with the blinds.*]

OFFICIAL: Have you ever had anyone famous?

PROSTITUTE: I can't tell you that.

OFFICIAL: Oh yes you can.

PROSTITUTE: No, I can't.

[*Instead of closing the blinds he only succeeds in opening them completely.*]

OFFICIAL: Oh no.

[*He steps back.*]

PROSTITUTE: If I do you won't trust me, so I shan't.

OFFICIAL: Here, can you do this? [*He sits down again.*] It's certainly true I don't want you telling anyone about me.

PROSTITUTE: Well I won't, don't worry.

OFFICIAL: But then, being the weasel I am—and we're all weasels now, aren't we?—I'd like to know about some of them.

PROSTITUTE: I can't.

[*She gets off the bed.*]

OFFICIAL: Come on. Tell me about the politicians, at least. They don't count. And maybe, who knows, it might be one I know. Wouldn't that be marvellous?

PROSTITUTE: I can't.

[*She reaches the window.*]

OFFICIAL: Look, if you want me here every Saturday you'll have to do better than that.

PROSTITUTE: That's blackmail.

OFFICIAL: Yes.

[*She looks out the window.*]

PROSTITUTE: Oh, all right. There's one here.

OFFICIAL: Where?

PROSTITUTE: Outside.

OFFICIAL: Outside?

PROSTITUTE: Yeah, come and look.

OFFICIAL: You're joking, a real politician you've had? [*He gets up and goes to the window.*] You mean him, that man running?

PROSTITUTE: Yeah.

OFFICIAL: In the trainers and tracksuit?

PROSTITUTE: Yes.

OFFICIAL: He's not a politician. He looks like a thug.

PROSTITUTE: That's Ten Rounds Milligan, that is. He counts, doesn't he? He's sort of on the fringes, isn't he?

[*She closes the blind. The room goes dark.*]

OFFICIAL: Good point—all right, he counts. Now, tell me all about him.

PROSTITUTE: You've perked up suddenly.

OFFICIAL: I have an interest in him.

[*She gets back on the bed.*]

PROSTITUTE: I stopped him, right.

OFFICIAL: You propositioned him? I thought that was illegal.

PROSTITUTE: Never mind about that. Just listen to the story. We agreed a deal. Quick sex and then he'd take me out for a drink. Remember the drink ...

OFFICIAL: All right.

PROSTITUTE: He did the business. We started talking. Now he's a psycho. You can't imagine he'd be interested in anyone else. Wrong. He wanted to know about me. Suddenly, I was looking forward to my drink. Then, next thing, he was going to take his Stanley to my nose. He was like a light switch. One minute nice as pie, the next, he was going to cut me.

OFFICIAL: You didn't tell him he'd a small cock, did you?

PROSTITUTE: Do you think I'm stupid?

OFFICIAL: Did he not want to pay?

PROSTITUTE: No, he paid.

OFFICIAL: So what was this all about?

PROSTITUTE: There was a smell off him you see. As a girl I remember it on my daddy's farm overalls. With yer man now it was far stronger, 'cos it was coming out his pores. So, not thinking of course, I said, 'You smell like my da.' He said, 'Any more of that crack, I'm going to take my Stanley to your nose.' Then off he stormed. So no drink for me.

OFFICIAL: I don't understand. This was all because you said he had a farm smell?

PROSTITUTE: No, don't you see? I'd caught him out.

OFFICIAL: No, I don't see.

PROSTITUTE: When you work with fertiliser, it gets under the skin. All explosives do.

OFFICIAL: When was this?

PROSTITUTE: Three weeks ago. [*He begins to search his pockets frantically.*] He thought I'd tout. That's why he threatened to take my nose off. That's why he broke his promise to take me for a drink. People are weasels—remember? They make promises and then they don't keep them. Are you all right? You've gone white.

OFFICIAL: I can't get a signal on my mobile. Where's yours?

[*She fishes her mobile out from under the bed and tries to turn it on.*]

PROSTITUTE: Oh no, flat battery. I meant to charge it last night. But with all the excitement I forgot. [*He bolts for the door.*] Where are you going?

OFFICIAL: I have to find a phone.

PROSTITUTE: Are you coming next Saturday or what? [*He is gone.*] Oh, all right, be like that. [*She is alone. She turns the television back on. On the soundtrack we hear a chat-show host.*] Now where's my make-up? [*She finds make-up and begins to put it on.*] Ten Rounds Milligan—I said ye smelt of fertiliser and ye got uppity. Well, someone believes me and not anyone but a clever man.

Mister NIO. I wonder will he be back next Saturday? [*She looks up.*] If I was to make a promise, would you give him to me? Please.
[*She closes her eyes and starts to pray.*]

Blackout. Explosion.